The Way of St Teresa of Avila

An Introduction

EUGENE McCAFFREY OCD

First published 2014 by:

TERESIAN PRESS
Carmelite Priory
Boars Hill
Oxford OX1 5HB
priory@carmelite.org.uk

ISBN 978-0-947916-15-2

A catalogue record for this book is available
from the British Library.

Cover design by Joshua Horgan, Oxford

Typeset and printed by Joshua Horgan, Oxford

For my Carmelite brethren
of the Avila Community, Dublin
and of all the other Carmelite communities
in which I have had the privilege to live

Contents

Preface

March 28, 2015 marks the fifth centenary of the birth of St Teresa of Avila. The occasion is a grace-filled invitation to explore and reflect on the legacy and teaching of one of the great women of the sixteenth century. Teresa has left an indelible mark on the history and spirituality of the Church, not only in her own time but for the past five hundred years. She is an incredibly gifted teacher, a persuasive writer, a sure spiritual guide and a woman of great charm and persuasion. Not without reason has she been ranked among the Doctors of the Church – the first woman to be granted this title.

The purpose of this small book is simply to provide a basic introduction to her writings. It is not intended as an in-depth study or analysis of her works. There are many excellent individual studies and commentaries available, both on her writings as a whole and on individual books.[1] My general aim has been to gather together into one small book the principal ideas found in larger and more scholarly works. I have found, over the years, that for many people the first question they ask is not: Where do I begin?, but: Where did Teresa herself begin? How did such a reluctant and unlikely writer create so many spiritual masterpieces and literary gems? My main intention has been to offer basic but essential information about the different books Teresa wrote, the reason why she wrote them, and the general content contained in each of them.

The writings of Teresa are a reflection of her own life and times. The first two chapters attempt to place her within the historical and social context of sixteenth-century Spain, so as to look at her family background and the cultural and religious climate out of which she wrote. In Chapter 3, we see how her personal style of writing developed. The fourth chapter then looks at the genesis of each book and the general ideas it contains, while the following one explores the historical and literary influences that shaped and formed these ideas. The final chapter offers an overview of some of the central themes and motifs that form the core of Teresa's teaching.

As a prelude to the discussion of her writings, I have included a brief Chronology, which may serve as a reference for the principal dates and events of her life. And at the end of this book, I list some other works, of larger scope, on the writings of Teresa, and which readers may wish to follow up.

In the closing chapter of her autobiography, Teresa reflects on how difficult the whole task of writing has been for her when she has so little time. Yet she adds: *the difficulty will have proved well worthwhile if I have managed to say something that may bring someone to praise the Lord, even if only once* (L 40:23). The more we read her writings, the more we are drawn into such praise, not only of the Lord but also of Teresa. Thanks to her, and to the personal cost and effort on her part, we can, five hundred years later, be nourished by her words of light and life, and find encouragement and inspiration in the sure guidance and practical wisdom of her teaching.

October 15, 2013
Feast of St Teresa of Avila

Chronology

Early Years: 1515-1536

1515   Teresa de Cepeda y de Ahumada born in Avila, March 28

1522   Teresa and her brother Rodrigo set out for the 'land of the Moors'

1528   Death of Teresa's mother, Doña Beatriz de Ahumada

1531   Teresa becomes a boarder at the Augustinian school of Our Lady of Grace in Avila (which she leaves in 1532 because of illness)

1533   Spends some time convalescing with her uncle Don Pedro in Hortigosa, and with her elder sister María in Castellanos de la Cañada

1536   November 2: enters the Carmelite convent of the Incarnation in Avila

1537   November 3: makes her profession as a Carmelite nun

1538   Teresa's health breaks down; goes to Becedas for treatment

       Reads Osuna's *Third Spiritual Alphabet*

1539   Returns, gravely ill, to her father's home; almost dies after four days in a coma

1540   Returns to the Incarnation, still seriously ill

1542   Teresa is cured through the intercession of St Joseph

1543   Death of Don Alonso, Teresa's father

1554   Teresa's total conversion to the Lord before a statue of the wounded Christ (during Lent). Beginning of her mystical experiences

1560   Receives the grace of transverberation

       Writes the first of her *Spiritual Testimonies*

1561   Around the end of the year, or the beginning of the next, starts to write the first version of the *Life*: completed in June 1562

Life as a Foundress: 1562-1582

1562   August 24: Foundation of St Joseph's, Avila

1563   Writes the *Constitutions* (approved in 1565 by Pius IV)

1565   Towards the end of the year, completes the second version of her *Life*

1566   Probably this year, completes the first version of *The Way of Perfection*, begun soon after finishing the *Life*, and possibly this year, also, writes the first version of *Meditations on the Song of Songs*

1567   Around this time, writes the second version of *The Way of Perfection*

       Visit to Avila of the Carmelite General, Juan Bautista Rubeo: permission is granted to extend the Reform

       Foundation of the second house of the Reform, in Medina del Campo

       First meeting of Teresa and John of the Cross at Medina

1568   Foundations of new monasteries of nuns in Malagón and Valladolid

       November 28: first foundation of the friars, at Duruelo

1569   Foundations of monasteries of nuns in Toledo and Pastrana

Probably at this time writes her *Soliloquies*

1570   Foundation in Salamanca

1571   Foundation in Alba de Tormes

Teresa is appointed Prioress at the Incarnation (October 1571-October 1574)

1572   Receives the grace of spiritual marriage

Sometime between 1572 and 1575, writes the second version of *Meditations on the Song of Songs*

1573   This year (or late 1572), writes *Response to a Spiritual Challenge*

Begins writing *The Book of Her Foundations* in Salamanca

1574   Foundation in Segovia. Returns as Prioress to the Incarnation, Avila

1575   Foundations in Beas and Seville

1576   Foundation in Caravaca

While in Toledo, writes *On Making the Visitation*

1577   Writes *A Satirical Critique* early this year (or at the end of 1576)

Writes *The Interior Castle*; starts it in Toledo in early June, and finishes it in Avila at the end of November

Imprisonment of John of the Cross in Toledo (December 1577-August 1578)

1578 Period of intense opposition towards the Reform

1580 Foundations in Villanueva de la Jara and Palencia

The Reform is granted its independence by a Brief of Gregory XIII (June 22)

1581 Writes the last of her *Spiritual Testimonies*

Foundation in Soria

1582 Foundation in Granada by John of the Cross and Anne of Jesus

Teresa makes her last foundation, in Burgos

Dies at Alba de Tormes on October 4

Posthumous

1614 Beatified by Paul V (April 24)

1622 Canonised by Gregory XV (March 12)

1970 Declared Doctor of the Church by Paul VI (September 27)

1982   Fourth centenary of her death

2015   Fifth centenary of her birth (centenary year celebrations: October 15, 2014-October 15, 2015)

The Writings of St Teresa of Avila

The Book of Her Life

Spiritual Testimonies

The Way of Perfection

The Interior Castle

The Book of Her Foundations

Meditations on the Song of Songs

On Making the Visitation

The Constitutions

Soliloquies

Response to a Spiritual Challenge

A Satirical Critique

Poetry

Letters

Teresa's writings
are a message of hope for everyone:
interested theologians, other religious,
and even atheists,
philosophers, psychologists, doctors…
Through her knowledge of the human heart,
she addresses herself to every person
of good will
in search of truth.

Jean-Jacques Antier[2]

Chapter 1
A Woman with a Mission

Teresa of Jesus, as she liked to be called, was born Teresa de Cepeda y Ahumada in the walled city of Avila, Spain, in Holy Week 1515. It was a time of turmoil and religious upheaval, not only in Spain but all over Europe. Ordinary people and Church leaders alike struggled to find a new identity for their lives in a rapidly changing world. Although it marked the Golden Age of Spanish literature and art, it was also an age of unprecedented turmoil and massive transformation as old certainties gave way to new discoveries and unheard-of exploration.

Whether she was aware of it or not, Teresa's life and her writings were shaped and influenced by the dramatic events taking place all around her. The invention of the printing press transformed the whole world of books and literature, and opened up a fascinating field of endless possibilities for the young Teresa; she became an avid reader, delighting in the romantic tales of chivalry, never happy unless there was a new one: *I was so completely taken up with this reading that I didn't think I could be happy if I didn't have a new book*

(L 2:1). It was a habit that stood her in good stead for her later years and fired her imagination with vivid, colourful images that adorn her writings.

Her family belonged to the prosperous merchant class; and her father, though not wealthy, was comfortably well off. In 1492 a vast horizon of colonial expansion opened up with the discovery of the Americas. The flower of Spanish youth left in their thousands for this 'new world', something Teresa experienced at first hand as eight of her nine brothers sailed to the Americas, seeking adventure and fortune, some of them never to return. The wealth of the colonies flowed back to the Spanish mainland, affecting social structures and giving rise to a prosperous middle class made up of builders, merchants and bankers, many of whom supported Teresa in her foundations; 'Avila of the Knights' had become, we might say, 'Avila of the Merchants'. When her favourite brother Lorenzo returned to Spain with his family in 1575, he was able to provide invaluable financial backing for the foundation of the Seville convent and remained a reliable support and a shrewd adviser in many of her undertakings.

Religious upheaval

However, it was the Protestant Reformation, a religious event of immense political and social importance, that most affected the life and work of Teresa. The Protestant Reformation both shattered Christendom and divided Europe. It was, in part, a reaction against the secular values and humanism of the times. But its deeper protest was against the corruption and decadence of the Church itself.

When Martin Luther and the handful of theologians who supported him made their famous statement of dissent in 1517, it was no more than a desperate cry for reform; but what started as a protest became a revolution and ultimately led to division and separation. Within the space of a single generation, the unity of the Church had been shattered and the political and social history of Europe dramatically altered.

Teresa was greatly distraught on hearing that *churches are destroyed, so many priests lost, and the sacraments taken away* (WP 35:3). In fact, it was the news of the ravages of Protestantism in France that would inspire her, in 1562, to establish her Reform and found her first monastery of strict observance, St Joseph's in Avila. *The news distressed me greatly, and, as though I could do something or were something, I cried to the Lord and begged Him that I might remedy so much evil* (WP 1:2).

The Protestant Reformation never gained a foothold in Spain: the soul of the Spanish people set itself against the new religion. More and more, as the century advanced, Spain became the spearhead of the Counter-Reformation and found in King Philip II a strong advocate of the Catholic revival. Philip also proved an invaluable ally to Teresa in her enterprise. She wrote several letters to him. He knew and admired her work, and she was fully conscious of his interest and patronage: *we would be lost, without the king's favour, for it is the king who supports and intercedes for us with the pope* (Lt 262:7). In the end his friendship proved invaluable, as it was largely through his intervention that in 1580 the Reform was established as a separate Carmelite province and given the freedom and independence it needed for survival.

A new heart, a new spirit

Throughout Europe in general, the Catholic reaction to the religious turmoil was at first slow and hesitant; only gradually did the Church set about putting its own house in order. In this regard, the importance of the Council of Trent (1545-1563) can hardly be overestimated. It became the rallying point for all the scattered forces of Catholicism and gave a firm basis of dogma and discipline to the work of renewal: through the Counter-Reformation, Catholicism received a new soul.

The impact of the Council penetrated deeply into the religious and political life of Spain. Teresa herself was profoundly affected by its influence. She had to take into account the decrees of the Council in the establishment of her convents. And in much of the opposition she experienced from 1575 until 1580, her enemies used the same decrees to attack her. The Papal Nuncio, Felipe Sega, openly condemned her as a 'restless, disobedient and contumacious gadabout, who, under the guise of devoutness, invented false doctrines, leaving the enclosure against the orders of the Council of Trent and her own superiors...'[3]

The teaching of the Council is echoed in the opening chapters of *The Way of Perfection* and the Epilogue of *The Interior Castle*; and the Council's decrees on justification and grace are given personal witness in Teresa's own life. Indeed, more than many of the learned doctors and theologians who took part in that historic Council, she could rightly be called the 'saint of Trent'. As Trent strove to renew the life of grace throughout the whole Church, Teresa gave all her energy to living as fully as she could this mystery of grace in the interior castle of her soul and in the life of the small community of nuns entrusted to her care. She understood holiness as sanctity in the service of the Church, and she reflected in herself the spirit of the reforming Church of her day, her one aim being to support, strengthen and build up the Church of Christ in whatever way was possible for her.

A service of love

It was in this century, then, that Teresa lived and wrote, and it is in this context that we must see her mission and writings, as well as her passion for the renewal of the Church and of the Carmelite Order. *I resolved to do the little that was in my power; that is, to follow the evangelical counsels as perfectly as I could and strive that these few persons who live here do the same. I did this trusting in the great goodness of God, who never fails to help anyone who is determined to give up everything for Him* (WP 1:2). Her tears, her prayers, her love for Christ and for his Church drove her to do whatever she could, in her own small way, to redress the havoc and disintegration she saw all about her. *The world is all in flames*, she cried; *they want to sentence Christ again, so to speak, since they raise a thousand false witnesses against Him; they want to ravage His Church...* (WP 1:5). His friends may be few, she realised, but they should be trusty ones.

She had found her life's work and mission. In an age of violent religious feeling and contrasting loyalties, her vocation became clear: to sow seeds of renewal, establish oases of prayer, and create communities of love and intercession for a fragile and embattled Church. Her writings and her teaching would reflect her dream for a world renewed, and for a Church purified by prayer and love in the service of her Lord.

Chapter 2
A Woman of Her Time

Teresa was naturally affected by the political and religious happenings of her day. We find some references, especially in her letters, to contemporary events, but her main concern, as we have seen, is with the recent troubles that were affecting the Church, and the harm and havoc being caused by those she described in general terms as 'Lutherans'. Her Reform was part of her personal response to the sufferings of the Church in her day and must be seen within the whole movement of the Counter-Reformation.

But Teresa was not only Spanish, she was Castilian; and the 'fire of Castile' burned in her veins. Castile was both the economic and spiritual capital of Spain. It had played a key role in the unification of the country, and its people were proud and noble in their military achievements. Teresa was Castilian not only in her good manners and personal graciousness, but also in her practical qualities of leadership and good government. Through page upon page of her writings, we find the same indomitable spirit and the same fearless resolve that characterised the knights and soldiers of her beloved Castile.

I have always esteemed virtue more than lineage

This free and independent spirit is clearly displayed in her reaction to the social attitudes of her day. Her *Life* and her letters, for example, show how deeply she rejected many of the accepted social structures of the time. Honour and 'purity of blood' were overriding obsessions with the nobility and upper class and were of fundamental importance in establishing relationship within society. They had their roots in the feudal system and were historically embedded in the cause of Spanish unity; over the centuries they had assumed both a religious and a political dimension. Teresa herself had little time for either: honour – *accursed honour* (L 31:23), she called it – was *the greatest lie* (L 20:26); and she never allowed 'purity of blood' to be a factor in accepting nuns into her convents. Had not Our Lord himself chided her during the foundation of Toledo? *He told me that lineage and social status mattered not at all in the judgment of God* (F 15:16).

The nature of society, as Teresa understood it, depended not on titles, wealth or status but on our relationship with God and on our love and friendship with each other. Her conversion, when it came, was not only spiritual, it would have social implications as well: her Reform was, in its own way, a rejection of empty and meaningless social distinctions. She simply replaced false honour with what was true and authentic, and we could easily miss the full impact of such a seemingly casual remark in her *Foundations*: *I have always esteemed virtue more than lineage* (F 15:15).

While always respectful in her dealings with people of noble rank, we find in her writings a disregard for social niceties and a certain sadness at their futility. For her, humility was the basic social virtue: the foundation not only of prayer and of our relationship with God, but of all human relationships. She was determined to remove from her convents not just the abuses of cloister she had witnessed at the convent of the Incarnation, which she had entered in 1535, but abuses within community life itself, such as preferential treatment and social distinctions based on dowry or family title. She was reluctant to accept into her convents women of high or noble rank, only doing so under circumstances outside her control.

Jewish background

Often as not, in sixteenth-century Spain, judgments and attitudes were more social than personal. Teresa and her family suffered much from such prejudice. Although she herself never referred to her Jewish background, of which she was surely aware, it was a social factor never forgotten. Her family belonged to an influential group of *conversos* or 'New Christians' – converts of Jewish extraction who had become Catholic, mostly under pressure from the Inquisition, though some secretly continued their practice of the Jewish faith.

In 1485 Teresa's grandfather Juan Sánchez, a cloth merchant, was obliged to perform public penance in Toledo, to re-establish his 'purity of faith'. After his reconciliation with the Church, he moved with his family to Avila and successfully continued his business there. But the stigma followed them. For four years (1519-1523), they were involved in an unseemly lawsuit to obtain a title of nobility, and therefore erase the presumed stain of Judeo-*converso* origin and settle the question of pure blood.

It seems impossible that the young, alert Teresa, who was eight years old at the time, could not have been aware of the controversy and the family's dark secret. Certainly it was well known in Avila and Toledo, for the tribunal's proceedings alternated between the two cities. New Christians were frequently regarded with resentment and suspicion; part of the opposition Teresa encountered during her foundations, and some of the more personal criticism of her activities, was inspired as much by social factors as by religious or spiritual motives.

Social challenge

Another area in which we see reflected the prevailing social climate of the day, and catch a glimpse of her family background, is in her material concern for her convents and her daily administration of the houses. It is interesting to note that not only was Teresa's reform mainly Castilian, it was also almost exclusively *urban*. All her life she was reluctant to establish convents in remote or rural areas. In this she was showing not only good practical judgment and concern for the welfare of her sisters, she was reflecting her own native instincts as well. Teresa's family, as we have seen, belonged to a tradition of merchants, bankers and businessmen – people who, in fact, supported and financed many of her journeys and foundations, and whom she was very happy to refer to as *my friends* (F 14:6).

Indeed, the more we read of her writings, the more we see that Teresa's relationship with the material world was almost as great as her relationship with the spiritual! In the *Foundations* and her letters, for example, we can see how heavily she was burdened with a thousand cares and concerns for her convents and for the sisters, as well as the endless worry that came to her from her own family and relations. Teresa did not need any supernatural visions to supply her with the images of gold, silver or diamonds which adorn her description of spiritual realities! When she spoke of virtue as the *current coin* (WP 18:7), she knew both the importance of virtue and the value of the current coin. And her concern with poverty – the *great walls* (WP 2:8) of her convents – was not only to emphasise its fundamental importance in relation to the religious life and the sisters' dependence on God, but also to safeguard a healthy independence from social and economic factors.

A new way

Finally, we see in Teresa a gathering together of many of the elements of the religious and spiritual movements of her time. She picked her way carefully through a maze of exaggerated and often dangerous extremes. She was only too well aware of the ever present and censoring eye of the Inquisition which published its infamous *Index of Forbidden Books* in 1559, and also imposed a ban on foreign books and on students studying abroad. Teresa herself was constantly under suspicion.

In 1575, *The Book of Her Life* was denounced to the Inquisition; it was confiscated and not released until after her death. In 1576, while she was in Seville, two Jesuits were sent to interview her on behalf of the Inquisition. She herself was unfazed by the visit and the happy result is two of her most precious *Spiritual Testimonies* (ST 58 & 59) which were written at their request. Teresa was also conscious of the tensions between the 'theologians' and the 'spiritual writers', and the mutual recriminations of both. Yet such was her genius that she could number many outstanding figures of each group among her closest friends and supporters.

Without compromise she was able to reconcile into a unity a whole new school of spirituality, founded on the bedrock principles of the best spiritual traditions. Despite opposition, misunderstandings and even condemnation, she created out of her own Reform, however humble its beginnings, a renewed and interior Christianity that did more to stem the tide of Protestantism than *the force of arms* (WP 3:1) advocated by some. In asserting the right of a handful of women to practise mental prayer, and to follow the evangelical counsels to the best of their ability and in their own particular way, she was asserting the right of all women to take their rightful place in the Church and to serve God in the joy and freedom of their own specific calling.

Teresa was not afraid to forge her own way or take the less travelled road: she reformed men and defended women; she walked with God yet never lost the common touch; she was a would-be solitary who became an intrepid traveller; a reformer and foundress, and an artless writer of literary and spiritual gems.

Chapter 3
Teresa as a Writer

As a writer, Teresa was unique. She was not an 'author' in the ordinary sense of the word: she preferred the spinning wheel to the quill! She was all too conscious of what she called her *rough style* (WP 16:13), her lack of time and her poor memory. She never set out to 'write a book' as such: practically all her writing was at the request of others. Her main concern was to describe her own experiences in prayer for her confessors or to instruct her Carmelite sisters in the way of prayer. Once she had completed this task, she felt she had fulfilled her obligation.

Nevertheless, she seems to have belonged to that privileged few who can truly be called 'born writers'. One's first impression on encountering her writings is surely just what a sensible woman she was, and how well she could say necessary things in simple and plain language. Her quickness of mind and sensitivity join with a ready wit to make her an intensely human writer and one of the most approachable of all Christian mystics. She had a keen intelligence and a creative imagination, coupled with that feeling for life and insight into people that is the quality of all great writers. Above all else she was rich in human qualities – friendship, compassion, rich humour and a basic common sense – and she could express divine as well as human truths in a manner that was clear and unaffected. There is a complete absence of artificiality in her writings; she is totally honest, and she combines passion and enthusiasm with utter simplicity and candour. Her naturalness, with the simple, homespun texture of her style, has delighted countless readers in every age since it first flowed so spontaneously from her pen.

A casual writer

As an almost casual writer of prose, Teresa never adopted a literary 'style' as such. Indeed, her particular genius stems from the fact that she wrote exactly as she spoke – artlessly and without any literary pose. Her writings often read like the unedited transcript of a recorded interview. Teresa's spontaneity gives a feeling of intimacy to much of her writing as well as, of course, explaining her tendency to digress or to repeat herself. While never dull or boring, she can, at times – and she herself would be the first to admit this – be difficult to follow!

With some writers it is possible to separate their teachings from their personality. Not so with Teresa: she *is* her writings. To read her is to know her. Practically every page bears the impress of her forceful and vivid personality. She wrote out of her own experiences; and the unique quality of her writings is that they reflect, in such a personal way, the richness of her own spiritual journey. Her writings are her life, a faithful testimony to her own dynamic spirit.

She was not concerned with spiritual theology as such, but with the life of the spirit as she experienced it. For her, 'theologising' was always secondary. Her writings are neither systematic nor scientific, and she never tried to camouflage her lack of knowledge. Nevertheless, her words have an authenticity about them; their directness and humanity capture the core of human experience. The ease and down-to-earth quality of her writing have made her one of the best and surest guides in the restless searching of the human spirit.

She wrote as she spoke

Teresa had very little preparation as a writer. Basically, she knew how to write – and little else! She was able to construct clear, straightforward sentences and express herself in language that was simple and direct, but she knew practically nothing of the art of writing. She was indifferent to the rules of grammar and syntax. She seldom used capital letters, question marks or full stops; her writings are almost completely without divisions or headings, and she constantly fell back on abbreviations. She wrote from popular speech in the Castilian dialect of the time, which she spelt phonetically, and her vocabulary was that of common usage. Teresa simply wrote sentences: her manuscripts are a mass of straightforward, continuous writing. Quite literally, she produced 'writings' rather than books.

Although she read a number of good spiritual books, it is difficult to assess to what extent they influenced Teresa's understanding of the spiritual life. Much of what she read was stylised and unintelligible to her, and a lot of it was out of keeping with her own character. Perhaps the exceptions were St Augustine's *Confessions* and the letters of St Jerome. Certainly, St Jerome's vigorous and direct style would have appealed to her, a style found later in her own letters; and her reading of the *Confessions* of St Augustine must have influenced her, consciously or unconsciously, when she came to write her own autobiography a few years later.

I am not meant for writing

Yet the fact remains that St Teresa had very little, if any, formal preparation as a writer. To be a great writer, something more than reading – even good reading – is necessary. This is especially true in Teresa's case, for she wrote from the book of her own experience. She did not turn to books for ideas or inspiration, and seldom referred to or quoted other writers. This makes her greatness as a writer all the more extraordinary: for not only were her ideas and experiences uniquely her own, but so too were her expression and formulation of them.

Teresa had no aspirations to be a writer and often expressed a deep-rooted repugnance about this, constantly referring to a host of obstacles and problems: the noises in her head, poor memory, lack of learning... She pleaded with Padre Gracián: *For the love of God, let me get on with my spinning and go to choir and do my religious duties like the other sisters. I am not meant for writing; I have neither the health nor the wits for it.*[4]

Yet, whatever the pressure and anxiety she experienced from her lack of training or formal preparation, it did not hinder the ultimate perfection of her work. Indeed, in some way, more than any other factor, this has contributed to one of the most endearing characteristics of her writing: its total freedom and spontaneity. Not only was Teresa free from the constriction of grammar and syntax; she was, much more importantly, free from any preconceived systems of ideas or particular schools of spirituality. She could express her own individual ideas and experiences creatively and in her own unique way, with an independence and originality that is the hallmark of genius.

Writing with both hands

Teresa generally wrote in her cell, not at a table or writing desk, but squatting on the floor at a small ledge under the window. She wrote with a quill pen and used a very good quality paper and ink – all of which she insisted must be from Avila – and this has contributed greatly to the excellent condition of the manuscripts. Much of her writing was done either early in the morning after Communion, or late at night with poor lighting and quite often after a busy day of work or travel.

Many witnesses attest to the fact that she wrote with great speed and tremendous intensity. Teresa herself said: *Would that I had many hands with which to write so that while putting down some of these things I wouldn't forget the others* (WP 20:6). She was constantly interrupted in her writing, and often there were long intervals – weeks, sometimes months – before she could resume. During the writing process itself, she never reread what she had written and hardly ever deleted or corrected anything.

For the most part, she wrote without adequate time for the formulation of her thoughts and ideas. She had no outline or plan. Her material was organised as she wrote, and flowed automatically from the general thrust of what she wanted to say. With Teresa the ground plan is only apparent after the work is completed. Often enough she herself was unaware, except in a general way, of the overall structure of the book: *I shall write of other things as the Lord inspires me or that might come to my mind; for since I don't know what I'm going to say, I cannot say it in an orderly way* (WP Prol. 2).

Once she had finished writing, however, Teresa realised the value of what she had written. She had a great writer's sense of achievement and a feeling of pride and joy in her work, hence her maternal solicitude for all her writings. She became her own editor – quite a critical one – and undertook the task of transforming her 'writings' into books. These were divided into chapters, with titles and headings added, corrections made and mistakes removed. It is important to stress the value and importance of the headings and titles given by Teresa to each of the chapters, as they represent her own judgment on the relative value of any particular section of the book. She even rewrote two of her major works, her *Life* and *The Way of Perfection*. Shortly before she died, she corrected *The Way of Perfection* several times before sending it to be printed.

I shall have to use a comparison

Teresa's writings are clear, colourful and imaginative; they are essentially concrete and practical. She abhors abstractions and technical terms. All her descriptions of spiritual realities are direct and down-to-earth – whether it is of prayer as a heart-to-heart conversation with God, or humility as walking in the truth. And she is a persuasive writer, with the rare ability to make the difficult seem possible, even easy. Although the ultimate demands of her *Way of Perfection* are as pressing as those of John of the Cross' *Ascent of Mount Carmel*, she combines them with a gentle and motherly patience, making allowance for all the fragile weaknesses and inconsistencies of human nature.

Teresa is an imaginative writer and constantly resorts to the use of simile and metaphor: *I shall have to make use of some comparison* (L 11:6), she says. Her writings teem with vivid illustrations and graphic metaphors – there are over four hundred of these scattered throughout her writings. Images of water, fire and light abound, as well as everyday illustrations of flowers, birds, animals, battles, journeys by land or sea, the beautiful metaphor of the silkworm, and the surprising and homely reference to the game of chess and the bullfight! They help her to organise and explain her thoughts, and they contribute flair and colour and so often a touch of humour to many of her ideas.

Some, like the great allegories of the *way*, the *castle* or the *garden*, provide the essential structure for her major books. Others, more casual and throw-away, are sprinkled across almost every page, adding wit and sparkle to many of her comments and observations: St Peter of Alcántara she describes as a man made out of the roots of trees; too many nuns in a convent are like lizards in a hole; distractions in prayer are worse than a pack of wild horses; prayer itself suggests the image of the tortoise or hedgehog hiding within itself; while the devil, when he is defeated, can only clap his hands to his head in frustration!

The genius of her life

But the real greatness of Teresa, of course, is not in her style or in her wit, but in her sanctity. Ultimately it is the genius of her own life, a life lived wholly and totally for 'His Majesty', that transforms every page of her writings. Teresa would certainly have made her mark as a woman and a writer in whatever walk of life she had chosen; but that life would not have been transformed with the brilliance of her sanctity or the radiance of her intimate friendship with God. And in the final analysis, it is this that matters.

Teresa was privileged, as few have been, to live and move in the presence of the living God revealed in the hidden depths of her own soul; to speak with him there, to hear divine secrets, and to share the intimate communion of divine life. Her writings are great – not for what they tell us of Teresa, but for what they tell us of God and of his dealings with each human soul. Teresa was given the grace not only to experience divine mysteries, but in a sense to stand back from them and to record what she had seen and heard.

In revealing the secret depths of her own spiritual journey, she unwittingly charted a pattern of divine intimacy that has guided others, in every age since, in the ways of the spirit. As she struggled to understand the things she experienced, she was able to record, with deep psychological insight, the moods and patterns of the human response under the direct action of God's guiding hand. The supports, the pitfalls, the dangers, the signs, the lessons so painfully learned and so masterfully recorded of her own spiritual journey, have now become the principles of discernment for all who walk the inner path of prayer and contemplation.

Chapter 4
What Teresa Wrote

In all, Teresa wrote thirteen 'books' – eleven works of prose, of varying length and importance, plus a number of poems and a large collection of letters. Her principal writings are: *The Book of Her Life* (her autobiography), *The Way of Perfection*, *The Interior Castle* (also known as *The Mansions*), *The Book of Her Foundations*, and *Meditations on the Song of Songs*.

Her other writings include: *Spiritual Testimonies*, *Soliloquies*, *On Making the Visitation*, *The Constitutions*, *Response to a Spiritual Challenge*, *A Satirical Critique*, *Poetry* and *Letters*.

Without dealing with each in detail, we can look at the general outline and purpose for which they were written.

The Life

This is Teresa's first major work. She was forty-seven when she wrote it. It is fundamental to any understanding of Teresa and gives an essential insight into her life and background. The book was first written at the request of the Dominican

Padre Pedro Ibáñez and completed in Toledo in June 1562; there seem to have been a number of copies of this first version, but none has survived.

At the request of another Dominican, Padre García de Toledo, she rewrote the whole book with many new details and fresh passages, including the treatise on prayer and an account of the foundation of the first convent of St Joseph's in Avila. She wrote it, according to herself, with many breaks – almost stealing the time, *because it prevents me from spinning* (L 10:7). This final text appears to have been completed towards the end of 1565. It was never intended for publication, but was for many years widely circulated in manuscript form until it was sequestered by the Inquisition in 1575; it was not released until 1588, six years after her death. This is the *Life* as we now have it. The original manuscript of this final version, in excellent condition, is one of the priceless treasures preserved in the Escorial Library in Madrid.

This is Teresa's autobiography, though not in the strict sense of the word; it is more spiritual testimony than biography. Like the Gospels, it is a book of narrative theology: she skilfully weaves the historical details of her life into the story of her spiritual journey. Essentially it is a book on prayer. It has rightly been compared to St Augustine's *Confessions* and, like it, transcends categories and speaks a universal language of the heart. She herself gave the book no title, simply calling it, in a letter to a friend, *mi alma* – 'my soul': *Remember,...I entrusted my soul to you* (Lt 10:2). In another letter she referred to it as the *Book of God's Mercies* (cf. Lt 415:1). As she recounts these mercies, she tells her story, confesses her infidelities, breaks forth in prayer, and describes the mystical experiences she unexpectedly received.

The book is divided into forty chapters. The earlier and later ones are mainly historical, telling of her childhood, her youthful dreams, her vocation, her early years in religious life, and the foundation of the first convent of the Reform. The central section of the book (Chapters 11-21) revolves around her famous allegory of the different ways of watering a garden. This is a comprehensive treatise on prayer that stands in its own right, a precious gem set against the background of Teresa's own spiritual journey and her growing intimacy with the Lord. The closing chapters of the book record further favours and mystical graces she received in prayer.

Some Teresian scholars, including the renowned Carmelite editor Padre Silverio, regard the *Life* as Teresa's greatest book,[5] but this distinction is generally accorded to *The Interior Castle*. However, there is no doubt whatever that it is a work of genius, a spiritual classic – all the more remarkable in that it is her first attempt to capture the largely uncharted world of mystical prayer. Since then, every writer on prayer has been indebted to her insights and observations, and to the clarity and precision with which she so vividly captures the agony and ecstasy of the spiritual quest. Teresa's *Life* is much more than a conventional biography: it is a book that inspires, nourishes, and sometimes overwhelms – as it did Edith Stein who, after one night's reading, famously remarked, 'That is the truth':[6] the truth of God that illuminates and transforms.

Spiritual Testimonies

These are best understood as a complement to the *Life*. There are sixty-five in all,[7] of varying length and importance, covering the period of her life from 1560 until 1581, a year before her death. The first three testimonies were written before Teresa completed her autobiography and can be seen as a foreword to it; while the remaining ones could be considered an epilogue to the *Life*, continuing the story with experiences that occurred after the autobiography was written. Some of the testimonies consist of just a few lines, or notes recorded from day to day; others are much more intimate and personal, outlining a particular grace or counsel she had received.

Many of these shorter accounts were written down at Our Lord's command (cf. ST 24). Others

– for example, the first three – were written for her confessors and are of considerable length and significance, describing her state of soul and further spiritual favours she has received. They also add some personal details and anecdotes not found in the autobiography: her ecstasy in Salamanca (cf. ST 12), her account of the spiritual marriage (cf. ST 31), and her personal vow of obedience to Padre Gracián (cf. ST 36). They are all written in the same vivid, direct style found in the *Life*, as she continually struggles to understand and clarify the abundance of favours and graces which so often overwhelmed her.

Up to around 1572, Teresa recorded these favours on loose pieces of paper, generally after Holy Communion, but from that time onwards she wrote them in a little notebook which has unfortunately been lost. The *Spiritual Testimonies* are, according to Padre Silverio, 'like fragments of precious stones that fell off while the jewel was being cut; they are but particles, yet with facets as brilliant as the stones of which they formed part'.[8] Together they provide a rich source of insights into Teresa's continuing journey, and her constant struggle to understand herself on the unexpected ways in which the Lord was leading her.

Autograph copies of some of the *Testimonies* exist.

The *little book* (cf. F 7:1), as Teresa called *The Way of Perfection*, was written at the request of the nuns who lived with her at St Joseph's, the first convent of the Reform, to teach them about prayer and contemplation. Her confessor, Padre Domingo Bañez, encouraged her to do so. It seems to have been started soon after the completion of the *Life*. She already states in the Prologue that she will not be following any preconceived plan but will record her thoughts as they come to mind (cf. WP Prol. 2).

The Way of Perfection is the most distinctly motherly and domestic of all her writings; and more than any of her other books, it contains the dynamic spirit which she wanted to impart to her Carmelite sisters. It is a manual of practical advice and solid instruction in the way of prayer and the practice of virtue.

The theme of prayer gives the book its basic unity. Chapters 1-3 deal with the Carmelite vocation: *the mode and manner of life proper to this house* (WP Prol. 1), and the apostolic value of contemplative prayer within the life of the Church. She constantly reminds her sisters of the value and importance of their calling: *O my Sisters in Christ... This is why He has gathered you together here. This is your vocation. These must be the business matters you're engaged in. These must be the things you desire, the things you weep about; these must be the objects of your petitions* (WP 1:5). Chapters 4-15 focus on basic Christian virtues – love for each other, detachment, and humility – which are the foundation of all prayer; this is a theme she develops further in the next part of the book, where she speaks more explicitly about the nature of prayer and contemplation (Chapters 16-26).

The last sixteen chapters are deservedly the best known of all her writings. They are built around her famous exposition of the 'Our Father' which Hoornaert claims 'is, perhaps, the most beautiful that has ever been written'.[9] In this prayer, Teresa says, *the Lord has taught us the whole way of prayer and of high contemplation* (WP 37:1). Each petition of the 'Our Father' opens up new horizons of friendship and intimacy with God as she masterly interweaves her ideas and teaching on prayer around the words of *the Master Himself who taught you this prayer* (WP 26:1).

It is here that Teresa speaks especially about the *prayer of recollection*, which is essentially a prayer of companionship, an awareness of a loving presence that can ultimately open the way to *perfect contemplation* (WP 25:2), about which the sisters had asked her to write (cf. WP 16:3). These chapters contain some of Teresa's most original ideas on prayer, as well as the most practical and helpful.

The Way of Perfection is now universally acknowledged as a classic of spirituality, its scope extending far beyond the small community of the ten or twelve sisters for whom it was originally intended. The book has been called '*The Teresian Gospel*', because 'just as without the Gospel there is no Christianity, so without the *Way of Perfection* there is no Teresian Carmel'.[10]

The ideas and images Teresa uses are part of everyday spirituality and have a global appeal. The book contains metaphors that are very much part of present-day spirituality. Prayer is described as an open road – *the royal road to heaven* (WP 21:1), she calls it – along which every Christian is invited to walk; this echoes the universal call to holiness proclaimed by Vatican II.[11] Contemplation is a journey towards *the fount of living water* (WP 19:2). And there is her vigorous call to persevere as faithful soldiers of Christ, fired with great desires and strong determination: *take my advice and do not stop on the road but, like the strong, fight even to death in the search, for you are not here for any other reason than to fight* (WP 20:2). Added to this is her spirited defence of women, which has a strong contemporary ring about it: *Since the world's judges are sons of Adam and all of them men, there is no virtue in women that they do not hold suspect* (WP 3:7) – little wonder this sentence was deleted by the frowning censor!

Happily there are two autograph versions of *The Way of Perfection* in existence, named after the places where they are kept:

(a) *Escorial manuscript*: written in about 1566 for the nuns who lived with her at St Joseph's, Avila. This earlier version of the work has a wonderful freshness and spontaneity about it. Its style is easy, intimate, colloquial, that of a mother talking to her daughters. It was subsequently divided into seventy-three chapters, of which only three have a title.

(b) *Valladolid manuscript*: written in about 1567[12] for the other Carmels of the Reform. Teresa felt the original draft was not suitable for general use and rewrote the book in a more formal style. Passages that seemed too intimate were removed, and she suppressed illustrations that seemed too trivial or domestic. Other passages were enlarged and developed, especially her treatment of the prayer of recollection. The number of chapters was reduced to forty-two, all of which were given headings. Some of Teresa's own charm and simplicity are lost in the revision, but there is an overall gain in clarity and precision. Most editions of the book now give both versions: much of the Escorial manuscript either embodied within the text or acknowledged within brackets or in italic type.

The Way of Perfection was the first of Teresa's major works to be published, and she was fully involved in the editorial process. She took great care in editing it; there are at least three manuscripts meticulously corrected by her, with hundreds of amendments and annotations. The book was published in Lisbon in February 1583, four months after her death.

The Interior Castle

This is St Teresa's masterpiece and crowning glory: a classic of spiritual theology, born from her own lived experience. Written in 1577, five years before she died, it is the most ordered and mature of all her works. At first, she was reluctant to write another book; she felt she had neither the time nor the wits to do so and would only be repeating herself like a parrot (cf. IC Prol. 2)! In the end, obedience won out; and the book, written at the request of Padre Gracián, was begun, appropriately on Trinity Sunday, while she was in Toledo; it was finished six months later at St Joseph's, Avila.

The manuscript was copied as she wrote it, earlier pages of the work in progress being transcribed by one of the nuns almost immediately; in this way, there arose at almost the same time both the autograph and the first copy. Yet these were the most troublesome and perilous months in the whole history of the Reform, and we know that Teresa was forced to abandon the book for at least two months and perhaps longer. In all, she was probably able to give less than three months to the actual writing of it – an extraordinary timescale for such an extraordinary work.

The Interior Castle is a complete survey of the contemplative life. Teresa is writing from a point of arrival, looking back over the whole sweep of the spiritual journey, outlining the interplay of growth and struggle, light and darkness, joy and desolation as she herself had experienced them. Its construction is extremely clear and simple, the image of the castle giving it a unity that is lacking in some of her other books: *a most beautiful crystal globe, made in the shape of a castle, and containing seven mansions, in the seventh and innermost of which was the King of Glory, in the greatest splendour, illumining and beautifying them all.*[13]

The language is direct and there are few digressions; witnesses attest to the fact that she wrote the book at great speed and with intense concentration. The style is more precise and accurate than in any of her other writings, as she herself acknowledged shortly after finishing the book: *It deals with nothing else but who [God] is; and it does so with more exquisite enamelling and decoration. The jeweller did not know as much at that time [when writing the Life], and the gold is of a finer quality* (Lt 219:8).

The Interior Castle draws together all the great Teresian themes into a synthesis. The abiding presence of God, the beauty and capacity of the human soul, friendship with Christ, the call to transcendence with its endless possibilities, and the need for total and absolute surrender – all these themes culminate in the final revelation of the mystery of the Trinity.

They are masterfully portrayed from the first mansion, that of *self-knowledge* (IC I:2:8), to that of the seventh, which she calls *the empyreal heaven* (IC VII:2:9), where the most secret things pass between God and the soul. Using the striking image of the silkworm, Teresa skilfully describes the transformation of the soul into the image and likeness of Christ: *the little butterfly...dies, and with the greatest joy because its life is now Christ* (IC VII:2:5). The last three mansions are linked by the symbol of marriage, which she uses to describe the ever deepening union between the Lover and the beloved: *like what we have when rain falls from the sky into a river or fount; all is water, for the rain...cannot be...separated from the water of the river* (IC VII:2:4). Here, the ultimate stages of the prayer (of union) dovetail into the transforming grace that she calls 'spiritual marriage'.

Teresa's original intention was to divide the book into seven sections – which indeed it is, on the face of it. But as she wrote, she realised that it was a castle of many rooms, so she subdivided each of these as she thought best, adding titles and headings. In the end, even she herself seemed overwhelmed by what she had discovered: *Although no more than seven dwelling places were discussed, in each of these there are many others, below and above and to the sides, with lovely gardens and fountains and labyrinths, such delightful things that you would want to be dissolved in praises of the great God who created the soul in His own image and likeness* (IC Epil. 3).

The autograph of *The Interior Castle* can be found in the convent of the Discalced Carmelites in Seville. This manuscript was restored and rebound in 1962, to mark the fourth centenary of Teresa's Reform.

The Foundations

This is St Teresa's account of the fifteen foundations made by her between 1567 and 1582.[14] The first nineteen chapters were written in 1573 and 1574, at the request of her Jesuit director, Jerónimo de Ripalda. In 1576, a further eight chapters (20-27) were added, this time at the insistence of Padre Gracián. Then came an interval of four years, before the writing of the final four chapters (28-31), which were written from 1580 to 1582, probably during the actual making of the foundations. This is certainly true of the last foundation of all, Burgos, which was completed just a few months before Teresa died. However, she also records elsewhere that she had already been encouraged by an inner voice to *write about the foundations of these houses* (ST 6).

Teresa gave the book no title, but even during her life it was referred to as *The Foundations*. She divided the book into thirty-one chapters and added their titles. The autograph copy, in a perfect state of preservation, is kept in the Escorial.

The Book of Her Foundations is one of Teresa's most endearing works. It is a book impossible to classify – a chronicle, a diary, a memoir, a family history, a fascinating travel guide. Within its pages we find, as Tomás Alvarez remarks, 'some one hundred important persons, colourful adventures, Castilian and Andalusian landscapes, social classes and religious hierarchies, muleteers and bishops, mystical ecstasies and financial problems'.[15]

At times, Teresa strays from the narrative to speak about prayer, to give some counsels to prioresses and to offer advice about particular problems in a community. Essentially, it is like a series of letters keeping her daughters informed about the progress of the Reform. It is written in a chatty, intimate style, full of delightful details and vivid pen-pictures of people she met along the way. This is a mother telling her daughters the story of each of the foundations, recounting the trivial as well as the great, regaling them with events both humorous and tragic, all the while reminding them of the importance of prayer and virtue and of the loving providence of God that has made it all possible. It stands as a personal testament to her burning love for Christ and her passion for the spread of his kingdom.

Meditations on the Song of Songs

This is a short book of meditations based on the Song of Songs. A lot of uncertainty surrounds its composition. Most Teresian scholars today believe that Teresa wrote the book twice: the first draft possibly as early as 1566 in Avila, and the second sometime between 1572 and 1575. She herself gave it no title, nor did she divide it into chapters or add headings; all this was done by Padre Gracián for the first edition of the book in 1611. He called it *Conceptions of the Love of God*, but in recent years a number of editors have changed the title to *Meditations on the Song of Songs*: as better expressing the nature of the book, and as more accurately reflecting the mind of Teresa who herself referred to it as *my meditations* (M 1:8).

Although Teresa says she wrote the book at the suggestion of one of her confessors, she obviously needed little encouragement to do so: she had a deep love for the Scriptures, especially the Song of Songs, and the book came spontaneously from her pen. She admits in the Prologue that *it consoles me to tell my meditations to my daughters* (M 1:8), and pleads that women should be allowed to enjoy the riches contained in the word of God and to reflect on such a sublime theme.

The book contains seven chapters and is essentially a prayerful reflection on some of the verses of the Song of Songs. This was an audacious venture in itself: openly to reflect on the most evocative love poem in the Bible! In many ways, it is a résumé of her favourite themes. It speaks of the beauty of Sacred Scripture: *one word of His will contain within itself a thousand mysteries* (M 1:2). Like all her writings, it is about prayer and finds in the words 'bride' and 'bridegroom' an invitation to the deepest intimacy of friendship and love: the Lover searching for the beloved. A large section of the book is given over to the nature of peace, distinguishing true peace from that which is shallow and false. In the final chapter Teresa returns to one of her favourite themes: the relationship between the love of God and the love and service of our neighbour.

The Song of Songs was a dangerous topic to explore, especially for a woman, and anyone who did so was automatically suspect. When she was in Segovia – probably at the time of founding the Carmel there in 1574 – another confessor, Diego de Yanguas, heard about the book and immediately panicked! In Spain, even vernacular translations of the Bible were included on the *Index of Forbidden Books*. The Inquisition had

already imprisoned the eminent scholar Luis de
León for his translation of the Song of Songs from
Hebrew into Castilian. Padre Diego told Teresa to
burn her *Meditations*, which she did. Fortunately,
unbeknown to her, her sisters had already made
secret copies of it! For this reason we do not have
the autograph copy of the book – nor, in fact, do
we possess the entire text composed by Teresa:
only authentic fragments.

On Making the Visitation

This little book was written at the suggestion
of Padre Gracián, as a help for 'visitators':
those appointed to make an official visitation
of convents – something which, following the
decrees of the Council of Trent, was now a
juridical obligation. Teresa wrote the book in
1576 – reluctantly: *beginning this work has been
the greatest mortification for me, and I have felt
a strong repugnance toward doing so* (MV 1).
The book has no chapter divisions but, unlike
most of her original manuscripts, it is divided into
paragraphs. It is addressed to Padre Gracián and
concludes with some personal recommendations
for him. The autograph copy is preserved in the
library of the Escorial.

It is a highly practical book, full of good
judgment, balance, and insight into human nature.
It offers the fruit of Teresa's own experience of

the religious life and of her understanding of the feminine psyche. She is mainly concerned that the visitator himself should be aware of, and try to understand, the practical problems and difficulties of the cloistered way of life. She recommends that he *should not make any decrees, unless the matter is serious... For the nuns could become so weighed down with decrees that, unable to observe them, they will also give up what is more important in the rule* (MV 20).

The history of the book is a painful episode in the publication of Teresa's writings. After her death, when Gracián had fallen out of favour, it lay hidden for over thirty years in the library of the Escorial; it was then published, in 1613 while Gracián was still alive, but without any reference to him. It took centuries for the injustice to be redressed: not until 1883 was the original text, as it came from Teresa, published in its entirety.

The Constitutions

In the papal Brief of 1562, issued for the foundation of St Joseph's, Avila, Teresa was authorised to draw up constitutions for the new community. This she did in 1563, and they were approved in 1565 by decree of Pius IV. In 1567, when the General of the Order, Fr Juan Bautista Rubeo, visited Avila, he also gave his approval to these *Constitutions* for any other convents that would be founded. However, it was a living text that grew and developed over the years as various visitators, and Teresa herself, adapted it to the needs of the new Carmels. With Padre Gracián's approval, she sought suggestions from her Carmels concerning changes to be made in the final version of this document.

Teresa saw the *Constitutions* as a simple extension of the Carmelite *Rule*, to which she refers seven times in the text. She insists especially on prayer and spiritual formation, an equal distribution of work and service, and an atmosphere of silence counterbalanced by two periods of recreation each day. She places love above authority, insisting that *all things should be done with a mother's love* and that the prioress *should strive to be loved so that she may be obeyed* (C 34). Neither the prioress nor any of the sisters should ever use the title 'Doña' (cf. C 30); and Teresa even suggests that the *Mother prioress should be the first on the list for sweeping so that she might give good example to all* (C 22). The *Constitutions* are written in clear and precise language; they contain the essential spirit and fundamental charism of Teresa's Reform. Characterised by a gentle firmness and a quiet strength, they reveal both her practical wisdom and her keen spiritual insight.

The autograph copy of these primitive *Constitutions* has been lost, but several copies of it were made. The final version was published in 1581, the year before Teresa died, with some minor alterations suggested by the Chapter of Alcalá. It was the first book of hers to be published.

Soliloquies

This is essentially a book of prayers: seventeen beautiful prayers or meditations written by Teresa in the precious moments after Holy Communion. It has been called 'the Teresian psalter', and these prayers have been printed in the form of psalms. Some editors refer to the book as '*Exclamations of the Soul to God*'. They stand apart from her other writings, as the only book written spontaneously and by her own choice. We do not know for certain when or where they were written; the date generally given is 1569 when she was in Toledo. No autograph copy of the *Soliloquies* exists, and Teresa does not seem to have given it any title, but many copies of the book were made during her life.

The *Soliloquies* do not follow any preconceived plan: they are brief but ardent outpourings of her great soul in prayer. They are all characterised by the same theme – a passionate longing for her Beloved, and a yearning for ever closer union with him: *O my delight, Lord of all created things and my God! How long must I wait to see You? What remedy do You provide for one who finds so little on earth that might give some rest apart from You?* (Sol 6:1).

Many of the prayers are filled with biblical references or allusions: especially to the Psalms, the Gospels, the Letters of St Paul and, of course, the Song of Songs. They enshrine the most passionate outbursts of love to be found in the writings of the mystics – 'white-hot embers', Padre Silverio calls them, 'from the fire of the Saint's love, which... can still enkindle the hearts of those who read them.'[16]

Response to a Spiritual Challenge

This is the response written by Teresa (probably around 1573) on behalf of the nuns of the Incarnation when she was Prioress there, from 1571 until 1574, to a 'spiritual challenge' issued probably by the Carmelite friars of Pastrana. As in a tournament between knights, the two teams challenged each other: Pastrana versus Avila!

We do not possess the text of the challenge from the friars in Pastrana, and we have only a small part of the response from the Incarnation. Only one page of the original copy written in Teresa's hand is preserved; this is in the Carmelite convent of Guadalajara. The document has hardly any literary or doctrinal value. Perhaps its chief merit is Teresa's own challenge to any friar who can put up with a superior who is *very wicked, vicious, gluttonous, and badly disposed to him* (RSC 28)!

A Satirical Critique

This small but delightful piece of writing is a 'judgment' given by Teresa on four commentaries submitted on the words *Seek yourself in me*, spoken to her by Our Lord when she was in prayer. It was written in Toledo around the end of 1576 or early the next year, at the request of the Bishop of Avila, Don Alvaro de Mendoza. The autograph copy is preserved in the Carmelite convent of Guadalajara.

The document is written in a playful, teasing tone as the four contestants each receive Teresa's 'judgment' on their efforts: Julian of Avila, chaplain at St Joseph's; John of the Cross, chaplain at the convent of the Incarnation; Francisco de Saledo, not long ordained; and her brother Lorenzo who had recently returned from Ecuador.

The contestants obviously took the challenge much more seriously than Teresa herself: *I love all the contestants... But I have no intention of saying anything good about what the contestants have written... All these gentlemen are so divine that they have lost by going beyond what was asked* (Sat Cri 1, 3 & 9)! Each of the replies, she says, has its faults: she fears she may have to denounce her friend Don Francisco to the

Inquisition; Julian of Avila, though he started well, finished badly; John of the Cross was too long-winded and anyway missed the point: *God deliver me from people so spiritual that they want to turn everything into perfect contemplation* (Sat Cri 7)! As for her brother, Lorenzo, all she can do is pray for him and forgive him for his lack of humility!

Poetry

Although Teresa herself never claimed to be a poet, many images and word-pictures in her prose have a poetic and lyrical quality about them. Even in her lifetime she was renowned for her verses. Julian of Avila records how, on one of their journeys, 'as she saw us all needing some recreation to cheer us up...she made up some charming verses for she was very good at composing religious poetry.'[17] In her *Life*, Teresa refers to herself as someone *who though not a poet suddenly composed some deeply-felt verses well expressing her pain* (L 16:4).

She seems to have composed many poems during her lifetime, but only thirty-one have come down to us. She gave them no title, and they are generally referred to by their first line. Very few of her poems can be dated with any certainty. Her first one, beginning *Oh Beauty exceeding / All other beauties!* (P 6), was composed around

1560, but almost all her other poems belong to the period of the foundations (1567-1582). Only in recent years have some autograph copies of her poems come to light.

Like the poems of John of the Cross, some of Teresa's are based on the popular love songs and ballads of the day which she must have heard in her youth or on her travels through the towns and cities of Spain. Some were written more as prayers and hymns than for any literary effect; others, on the occasion of a community feast day or special celebration. They vary in style from shepherd songs and love poems of special beauty to artless hymns and simple rhymes.

A number of the poems express some deep mystical experience. As Teresa comments, in the *Life*: *Oh, help me God! What is the soul like when it is in this state! It would want to be all tongues so as to praise the Lord* (L 16:4). Others are playful and mischievous, like the verses about the *nasty creatures* (P 31): an infestation of fleas that invaded the rough woollen habits of the nuns! The poems easily lend themselves to music, and it is not hard to visualise Teresa herself merrily leading the dance to the ringing sound of the castanets! Included among her poems is her best-known and inspirational verse, found in her breviary after her death and now known as her 'Bookmark': *Let nothing trouble you... / God alone suffices* (P 9).

All in all, Teresa's poems are yet one more expression of her humanity, and a precious testimony to the joy and exuberance of spirit that so delighted those who had the privilege of knowing her. Her poems also established a tradition that has continued through the centuries: that of celebrating the lived experience of Carmelite spirituality in music, song and poetry, a tradition that has found full expression in the poems of Thérèse of Lisieux, Elizabeth of the Trinity, Edith Stein, and the American poet Jessica Powers. In this context Tomás Alvarez aptly refers to the famous remark of the philosopher Jacques Maritain: 'St Teresa used to say that even for contemplatives life would be unbearable if poetry did not exist.'[18]

Letters

Teresa wrote countless letters, perhaps thousands! The five hundred or so that have come down to us are only a fraction of the whole. They provide a rich insight into her life, as well as being a significant historical record of the period. Sadly, many of her letters have been lost or destroyed, including those written to Pope Pius V, Peter of Alcántara, Francisco Borgia, Julian of Avila and John of the Cross. All but five of her surviving letters belong to years associated with the foundations, as she kept in touch – often daily – with her Carmelite sisters and friends.[19]

Most of her letters were written far into the night by the light of an oil lamp, often after a long day of business or travel. At the top she put the initials 'JHS' in large letters. All her letters were signed, quite simply, 'Teresa of Jesus' and sealed with her own seal. Often, Teresa dated her letters only by the day or feast day; sometimes by the month as well; and she only gave the year when writing to America.

Teresa did not write all her letters in her own hand, certainly not after Christmas 1577 when she broke her arm in a fall and was suffering from exhaustion. From that year on, they were mostly written by her faithful and beloved companion Anne of St Bartholomew. Teresa used the ever available muleteers for most of her correspondence. Before sending her letters, she would fold the paper in such a way that the contents could not be read. The postage was agreed beforehand, but the full postage was paid only on receipt of the letter. Occasionally, for extra security, she used the royal mail, which was safer but more expensive.

Teresa kept in constant touch with her convents through her letters but she also wrote to relatives, friends and a whole gallery of helpers and supporters. The range of recipients is itself astonishing: persons in high society, from King Philip II to the Grand Inquisitor; numerous letters to nuns, priests and confessors, as well as to her own family, especially her brother Lorenzo; and the largest collection of all (no fewer than one hundred and fourteen) to her soul-friend Padre Jerónimo Gracián.

The letters are not strictly 'spiritual'. They generally deal with business affairs and everyday events. Some are of great importance, such as those on the defence of the Reform and the establishing of houses; others are more prosaic: concerns about finances, hiring workmen, appeasing landlords, even down to ordering food and gathering herbal remedies and cures for her sisters!

Letters were Teresa's natural medium. Every letter is a conversation – often animated, always personal and direct, never dull. They reveal her personality: in a sense, to know her one has to read her letters. There, we see her at her best: practical, patient, worried, teasing, sparkling with laughter and wit. Whether she writes to the Bishop, to her confessor, to her sisters, or to any one of her countless acquaintances, she writes with a deeply human touch and with an obvious love and affection for others. Although she loved to receive letters, writing them wearied her. *The biggest burden is letter-writing* (Lt 39:1), she tells her sister Juana; and we sometimes get the impression that she found the task even more exhausting than writing a book!

In her letters we see the extraordinary grasp she had of every detail of the Reform; but we also realise the enormous toll which her conflicts with those in authority, and the daily concern for her convents, had on her health. She is always on the watch: enemies are everywhere and friends sometimes let her down. She frequently takes the precaution of using pseudonyms in case her letters should fall into the wrong hands: she refers to herself as 'Angela', Gracián as 'Paul', and John of the Cross as 'Seneca'; the Discalced friars she calls 'eagles'; and the nuns, 'butterflies'!

But perhaps the chief value of her letters, apart from this deeper human insight we get into Teresa and her work, is the fact that here we see a woman – a mystic and a saint of God – who, for the last ten years of her life, lived in such intimate friendship with God and yet was so completely taken up with the everyday cares and worries of life, as she reveals herself in a manner so utterly human and practical. Her letters are surely one of the greatest commentaries in the history of spirituality on how grace perfects nature and transforms every human quality into service of God.

Chapter 5
A Living Book

.†.

It is always important to keep in mind the relationship between Teresa's writing and her personal experience. As said before, her writings are herself; every line expresses something of her inner journey, something living and practical, linked with life, especially her own. Her writings did not evolve in a vacuum: they were conditioned by the circumstances and situations in which she found herself. It is remarkable how many providential influences – saints, theologians, writers, and spiritual movements – came together for her, each helping her to deepen and clarify her thoughts and ideas.

Teresa had a naturally quick and enquiring mind. Her sensitive and sociable nature disposed her to make the most of whatever influences came her way. Her thirst for knowledge and truth, and the sheer profusion of the mystical graces she received, forced her, as it were, to seek guidance and enlightenment. As her understanding developed, so too did her confidence and maturity: she learned to discern more accurately the truth and falsity of what she read and heard.

I was very happy with this book

From her youth, Teresa was an avid reader. With a mixture of curiosity and thirst for knowledge, she devoured whatever books she could find in her father's library. In her cell in the convent of the Incarnation, she kept the religious bestsellers of the day; and later, when she came to write her *Constitutions*, she included a list of good books which she felt should be available to the sisters: *This sustenance for the soul is in some way as necessary as is food for the body* (C 8).

Two works, especially, had a decisive influence on her spiritual development. *The Third Spiritual Alphabet* by Francisco de Osuna was her favourite spiritual reading for many years. This book, which she read in about 1538 at the beginning of her religious life, was a revelation to her. Osuna was her first teacher in prayer, and the first to show her the relationship between prayer and love. It was here for the first time that she learned about the prayer of recollection, which was to be so much part of her own teaching on prayer: *I was very happy with this book and resolved to follow that path with all my strength* (L 4:7). It encouraged her to pray in a way that was free and personal; and she returned to it again and again, especially in the early stages of contemplation which were a period of such anxiety and confusion for her.

The same is true of *The Ascent of Mount Sion* by Bernadino de Laredo, which she possibly read in around 1554, underlining passages and marking phrases in an effort to understand the unexpected flood of mystical favours she had received. In both of these books she found what she was looking for at the time: clarity, direction and encouragement.

Sacred Scripture

As regards Sacred Scripture, Teresa never read the whole Bible. She knew no Latin, and translations in Spanish were limited and restricted. Our Lord, she admits, often came to her rescue: *without understanding the vernacular meaning of the Latin my soul is stirred and recollected more than by devotional books written in the language I understand* (M Prol. 1). Her knowledge of Scripture came mostly through the liturgy, partial translations, and quotations from spiritual writers; the *Life of Christ* by Ludolph of Saxony, one of her favourite books for meditation, was a rich source of Scripture for her.

Teresa confesses to a great love of Scripture, from which she quotes freely if not always accurately. Our Lord himself impressed this truth on her: *all the harm that comes to the world comes from its not knowing the truths of Scripture in clarity and truth* (L 40:1). She herself quotes the Scriptures nearly two hundred times. Over half of these quotations come from the New Testament – in particular, St John's Gospel and the Letters of St Paul; the rest are mostly from the Psalms and the Song of Songs. Indeed, as with John of the Cross, the Song of Songs was one of her favourite books; and as we have seen, she wrote a commentary on some of its verses.

People were astounded

It is important to remember that, when she wrote her *Life*, Teresa's ability to understand and express her experiences was still tentative and cautious. Even her ability to express them in clear, simple statements was a slow and painful process. All her life she was conscious of the fact that she was trying to express the inexpressible; but in those early years, the task was well-nigh impossible for her.

This was all part of the tension and anxiety between herself and her confessors, and a source of a good deal of misunderstanding on both sides. Only gradually did she become conscious of the fact that God himself was teaching and guiding her: *For it is one grace to receive the Lord's favour; another, to understand which favour and grace it is; and a third, to know how to describe and explain it* (L 17:5). Not only had he given her such an abundance of experience in prayer, but he was now also giving her the ability both to understand these experiences and to express them in writing: *although I spoke with many spiritual persons who wanted to explain what the Lord was giving me so that I would be able to speak about it, my dullness was truly so great that their explanations benefited me neither little nor much... Without my desiring or asking..., God gave me in a moment completely clear understanding so that I knew how to explain His favour in a way that amazed me more than it did my confessors* (L 12:6).

Not only did her literary style gradually improve, but there also came a facility to organise and structure her thoughts. This is discernible, for example, in the development of her three major works. Her *Life* is, in a sense, the least structured of all her writings. *The Way of Perfection*, on the other hand, comes closer to being a treatise on the spiritual life; it has the in-built unity of a practical handbook of prayer and spiritual instruction. *The Interior Castle* is, without doubt, the most unified and tightly knit of all her books; there is a flow and continuity about it, and the literary elements are totally subjected to the doctrinal and mystical dimension.

Finding solutions

Teresa was an original writer who absorbed influences into her bloodstream and welded them into a living synthesis. She did not make a

77

conscious effort to recall the ideas or thoughts of others. She did not read for 'ideas' or 'theories', but for practical solutions to her own problems; she sought guidance and enlightenment on concrete and particular situations. Nothing ever influenced Teresa as a teacher which did not first influence her as a person: *I shall say nothing about what I have not experienced myself or seen in others* (WP Prol. 3). Her life was her criterion; and her own personal, living relationship with the Lord was the only model by which she judged the value and worth of what she read and wrote.

It is also important to note in Teresa a gradual development in her understanding of the *psychological dimensions* of the spiritual life. Time and time again, she averts to the pain and confusion caused by her not understanding basic terms and distinctions that are the foundation of all spiritual theology: *These matters are expounded in mystical theology; I wouldn't know the proper vocabulary. Neither do I understand what the mind is; nor do I know how it differs from the soul or the spirit. It all seems to be the same thing to me...* (L 18:2).

It was only through trial and error, as well as much reflection and discussion with theologians, that she came to understand and accept many of these truths. Words and concepts like 'soul', 'spirit', 'mystical', 'natural' and 'supernatural' only gradually became clear to her, and she is ever at pains to share this discovery with her readers. Through her own experiences and her ever increasing facility to describe them, she has contributed immensely to our understanding of the human foundations of the spiritual life and the psychological fabric of the soul under the influence of transforming grace.

His Majesty has always been my Master

Of great importance is the direct influence of Christ, of whom Teresa could quite confidently say: *His Majesty has always been my Master* (L 12:6). Her relationship with him was of much greater significance than anything she read in books, and without this she is convinced that she would have understood nothing at all: *I had no master and was reading these books in which I thought I was gradually coming to understand something. (And afterward I understood that if the Lord didn't show me, I was able to learn little from books, because there was nothing I understood until His Majesty gave me understanding through experience, nor did I know what I was doing.)* (L 22:3).

Teresa was greatly distressed when the Inquisition published its infamous *Index of Forbidden Books* in 1559, but Our Lord comforted her with the words: *'Don't be sad, for I shall give you a living book'* (L 26:5). And so it happened: *the Lord showed so much love for me by teaching me in many ways, that I had very little or almost no need for books. His Majesty had become the true book in which I saw the truths. Blessed be such a book that leaves what must be read and done so impressed that you cannot forget!* (L 26:5).

Sources of influence

Sixteenth-century Spain was a ferment of intense spiritual revival; prayer groups and religious movements abounded. Not all were of the same thinking, and often a basic rivalry existed between them. Despite tension and rivalries, Teresa kept her balance and was generally happy with the particular emphasis of each group on the importance of prayer, simplicity, poverty and the practice of virtue; but she strongly rejected the extreme asceticism found in some of their followers.

Teresa's whole training and spiritual formation was essentially Carmelite. Whatever defects may have existed in discipline or community life in the convent of the Incarnation, the formation and spiritual training, both in liturgy and in prayer, was basically Carmelite. Apart from this, the two most significant Carmelite influences in her life were Jerónimo Gracián and John of the Cross. From 1576 onwards, Padre Gracián was her closest guide and confidant. His influence was mostly practical, and it was as mother and superior to an ever increasing number of houses that she turned to him for support and counsel during those last troubled years of her life.

The influence of John of the Cross was more profound, yet not always easy to determine. Of their mutual esteem and admiration for each other there is no doubt; yet in temperament and character they were very different. He seems to have been providentially placed to guide her through the later stages of the mystical life. His influence is apparent in the clarity and precision with which she was able to describe the final development of the mystical life in her masterpiece, *The Interior Castle*.

Among the other religious Orders, the most important for Teresa's personal journey were the Dominicans and the Jesuits. During her life she came into contact with no fewer than fourteen Dominican and ten Jesuit theologians. The Dominicans helped her to clarify her understanding of the principles of the spiritual life; the Jesuits, for the most part, supported her in practical issues concerning her own life. All in all, their influence was important and can, perhaps, best be seen in the facility with which she herself was eventually able to understand her own experiences and write about them.

Teresa was a born writer; of that there is little doubt. But this does not take away from the fact that she was enriched by those to whom she spoke, by the books she read, and by the many religious and literary movements she encountered. As she grew in confidence and wisdom her writings, too, like her friendship with Christ, became 'living books'.

Chapter 6
Selected Themes

Teresa was not an orderly or systematic writer. She did not have a 'theory' of the spiritual life; her writings were mostly spontaneous, dictated by her own experiences and the day-to-day situations that she encountered in her convents. Still, it is possible to see a number of central themes running through her writings, and it may be helpful here to outline some of them.

There are common elements found in all great spiritual writing: the following of the Gospel, the imitation of Christ, the dignity of our Christian calling, the importance of prayer. These are all there in Teresa's writings, but to each she has given her own particular emphasis, while some she has developed in a uniquely personal and creative way.

1. God alone suffices

Without any doubt, the central theme running through all of Teresa's writing is an overwhelming sense of the *reality of God*. His presence in her life was real and immediate, as was her awareness of his goodness and overpowering love. From the moment God called her, Teresa returned love for love.

We can, of course, say that all Teresa's writings are about prayer, but only in the sense that they are first and foremost about God: for prayer is that mysterious world of the spirit where our relationship with him takes place. Her witness is to the reality of the *spiritual world*, in which God is encountered as a living God – personal, close and loving, and who is intimately involved in the realities of our human existence. God was as real to Teresa as the prelates and magistrates, innkeepers and muleteers she encountered on her travels; angels, demons, saints and sinners moved easily in and out of her world as messengers of the supernatural.

Teresa did not find God: he found *her*. He had literally fallen upon her, taken possession of her life, and called her into deep intimacy and friendship with him. Her existence, in a real sense, is bound up with his and cannot be explained apart from him. God was her All: she not only lived *for* him, she lived *in* him and *with* him. There are almost nine thousand references to God, in one way or another, in her writings – not just an interest, surely, but an overriding passion and obsession! The reality of God became the reality of her life: the truth about God, the truth about herself. *God alone suffices* (P 9).

Her writings are a record of how this

transformation took place – all part of her testimony to the 'mercies of God'. For her, it was a progressive discovery, a gradual surrender; and to each new level of awareness she responded with ever increasing wonder and gratitude: *I often marvelled to think of the great goodness of God, and my soul delighted in seeing His amazing magnificence and mercy. May He be blessed by all...* (L 4:10). At its highest point, this became an almost uninterrupted awareness of the Trinity present in the depths of her soul. But its beginnings were painful and frightening, aggravated by her own resistance, the misunderstanding of confessors, and her constant fear of delusion and deception.

Yet the truth gradually became clearer and, in the end, impossible to deny: God was personally and immediately present to her, sharing her life and calling her to ever deeper friendship. Whole new vistas opened up: the majesty of God, the beauty of the soul, the depth of the divine intimacy, the wonder of prayer, and the personal presence of God in all created things: *Oh, our Emperor, supreme Power, supreme Goodness, Wisdom itself, without beginning, without end, without any limit to Your works; they are infinite and incomprehensible, a fathomless sea of marvels, with a beauty containing all beauty, strength itself!* (WP 22:6). The God she discovered within was a creative God, living and dynamic.

For Teresa, God and the things of God became the central truth of her life. This is the fundamental witness of her writings. *All is fleeting, / God alone is unchanging* (P 9). She found God who had found her – and she became, in her own words, a *servant of love* (cf. L 11:1).

2. The Good Jesus

According to Teresa, the name of Jesus was never far from the lips of St Paul. The same could be said of Teresa herself. Every saint, in one way or another, has found their way into the heart of Christ and fallen in love with him. Teresa was no exception: she never wrote a treatise on Christology, but she came to know the extravagance of his love at a personal level, and the overwhelming power of his call. How utterly simple are her words: *I had been so devoted all my life to Christ* (L 22:4). Christ was at the very heart and centre of every stage of her spiritual journey, guiding her all the way to the higher reaches of contemplation and beyond.

She cultivated a love for Christ through meditation on her favourite gospel passages, especially those where she felt he was most alone, such as in the garden of Gethsemane, in his passion; she loved to place herself at his feet with the Magdalene, or at the well with the Samaritan woman. Teresa's encounter in 1554 with a statue of the wounded Christ (cf. L 9:1) was a turning point in her life.[20] It was the first of a series of extraordinary graces that drew her ever more deeply into the mystery of his love.

A flood of visions and spiritual favours followed, each revealing more and more the 'unsearchable riches of Christ' (Eph 3:8). Her deepest and most loving insights were into the mystery of the Incarnation, the Word made flesh – Jesus as both God and man. As the full splendour of the Sacred Humanity was revealed to her, she was more and more overwhelmed by his exquisite beauty, a beauty she *would be unable to exaggerate* (L 28:1). She did not see Christ with the eyes of the body but far more clearly – with those of the soul: *If I should have spent many years trying to imagine how to depict something so beautiful, I couldn't have, nor would I have known how to; it surpasses everything imaginable here on earth* (L 28:4). He became for her, in all truth as he had promised, 'a living book'.

In him she found the fulfilment of all her searching, the model of what her own life should be, and the source and fountain of all grace. In speaking of Christ, Teresa uses every word she can think of to express the passion and intensity of her love. *This Lord of ours is the one through whom all blessings come to us. He will teach us these things. In beholding His life we find that He is the best example. What more do we desire than to have such a good friend at our side, who will not*

87

abandon us in our labours and tribulations, as friends in the world do? (L 22:7). He is especially the 'Good Jesus', but with a myriad of familiar faces: always His Majesty, her King and her Lord; but equally a brother, friend, guide, spouse, companion and teacher. Mystery and friendship converge and overlap without loss of intimacy.

Witnessing to Christ

Without keeping our eyes fixed on Christ, as Teresa did, we cannot understand her life or her teaching. His presence permeated her whole being, not just during prayer but in the midst of her busy life with all its difficulties, struggles and trials. Often he revealed his presence to her in the everyday events of life, spoke a word of comfort or enlightenment and let her know, in countless little ways, of his guiding and protecting hand. In the end, the transforming experience of her life, the grace of 'spiritual marriage', which took place in 1572, came through a most delicate and intimate exchange of love: the Bridegroom had come to claim his bride, and to set the seal on a love foreshadowed and now fulfilled in the haunting images of the Song of Songs.

Teresa's writings stand as a powerful witness to the authentic Christian tradition that whatever road one travels, the only true way is through Christ. It is also a powerful statement, against many of the 'learned men' (cf. L 22:2) of her day, that the humanity of Christ cannot, and must never be, bypassed in the flowering of contemplative prayer or in the most exalted mystical states. *Many, many times have I perceived this truth through experience. The Lord has told it to me. I have definitely seen that we must enter by this gate [of the sacred humanity of Christ] if we desire His sovereign Majesty to show us great secrets* (L 22:6).

Teresa's witness is all the more poignant because of her once mistaken belief that it could somehow be otherwise: *At no time do I recall this opinion I had without feeling pain; it seems to me I became a dreadful traitor – although in ignorance* (L 22:3). Here we see a practical humility, one that wants no other way than the one given by God himself; and she says, with a sane common sense and a realism that accepts the givenness of the human situation: *we are not angels but we have a body. To desire to be angels while we are on earth – and as much on earth as I was – is foolishness... Such has been my experience; it's the way God has led my soul* (L 22:10.11).

3. The door to the castle

Teresa's understanding of prayer, then, came from her experience of Christ. Her relationship with him was essentially one of friendship; and at its deepest level, she understood prayer as 'friendship with Christ': *Represent the Lord Himself as close to you and behold how lovingly and humbly He is teaching you. Believe me, you should remain with so good a friend as long as you can* (WP 26:1). Prayer is indeed a loving conversation, yet one in which words are not essential; sometimes, not only words but even thoughts are impossible. It is the relationship that matters, a relationship of ever deepening possibilities and new horizons.

The backdrop to Teresa's teaching on prayer is her famous description, given in *The Book of Her Life: prayer...is nothing else than an intimate sharing between friends; it means taking time frequently to be alone with Him who we know loves us* (L 8:5). This is an invitation to enter into an abiding and personal friendship with the one who we know loves us – keeping him company, talking to him often, in a heart-to-heart conversation: *the door of entry to this castle is prayer and reflection* (IC I:1:7).

But the relationship is twofold: the journey can be said to be as much God's as it is ours, and Teresa continually stresses the work of the divine Artist in our lives. Her image of the garden (cf. L 11:6) skilfully illustrates the interplay between perseverance and grace: dry soil can only come to life by watering – first by toilsome effort, then by waterwheels and running streams; but in the end, it is the sweet rain of God's gentle grace, often

90

coming when it is least expected, that produces fruit and flowers. All is grace and blessing.

For Teresa, prayer is not a pious exercise. It is an attitude to life. Even more, it is a way of life. She was not particularly concerned about the mechanics of prayer, which can often confuse rather than help: *When I see souls very earnest in trying to understand the prayer they have and very sullen when they are in it – for it seems they don't dare let their minds move or stir lest a bit of their spiritual delight and devotion be lost – it makes me realise how little they understand...; they think the whole matter lies in these things* (IC V:3:11).

It is friendship and personal relationship with God that matters, a loving and intimate communion to which we are invited. Her writings are indeed a sure and lucid guide to the working of God's transforming action in the human heart as she outlines the awesome journey of grace towards the fountain of living water that flows within. *Well, believe me; and don't let anyone deceive you by showing you a road other than that of prayer* (WP 21:6).

Prayer of recollection

Teresa writes of prayer at many levels: vocal prayer, prayer of recollection, contemplative prayer, and prayer of union. But it is the prayer of recollection that most fascinated her. Today, the same form of prayer is associated with a number of Christian writers, including John Main, Anthony de Mello and Thomas Keating, and is essentially the way of prayer practised in Christian meditation groups. *This prayer is called 'recollection', Teresa says, because the soul collects its faculties together and enters within itself to be with its God* (WP 28:4).

In fact, she admits that until the Lord taught her this way of prayer, she did not know what it was to get comfort out of prayer! *I confess that I never knew what it was to pray with satisfaction until the Lord taught me this method* (WP 29:7). And her words will certainly ring bells for many people when she claims it is a way of prayer that will have a special appeal for *those...who cannot engage in much discursive reflection with the intellect or keep [their] mind from distraction* (WP 26:2).

For Teresa, the prayer of recollection is a prayer of presence: an awareness of God hidden *within this little heaven of our soul* (WP 28:5). The whole dynamic is towards simplicity and personal relationship: *the teacher is never so far from his pupil that he has to shout, but he is very close* (WP 24:5). It is a prayer of companionship flowing from an open and attentive heart: *However softly we speak, He is near enough to hear us. Neither is there any need for wings to go to find Him. All one need do is go into solitude and look at*

Him within oneself (WP 28:2). It is a prayer of love, silence and listening, not a prayer of many words: *I'm not asking you now that you think about Him or that you draw out a lot of concepts or make long and subtle reflections with your intellect. I'm not asking you to do anything more than look at Him* (WP 26:3).

As always, for Teresa *the important thing is not to think much but to love much* (IC IV:1:7; cf. F 5:2). From her own experience, she is prepared to give the prayer of recollection her full endorsement: *Once this recollection is given by the Lord, you will not exchange it for any treasure* (WP 29:7).

Contemplative prayer

One of the characteristics of Carmelite prayer is its openness to contemplation. Indeed, it is precisely this quality that most attracted Teresa to the prayer of recollection. She sees it as the link, the bridge, that opens the heart to receive the greater and more purifying graces of contemplative prayer.

The Carmelite Reform was established precisely to create a way of life that would make contemplative prayer possible. Her concern for the smaller community and simplicity of lifestyle was essentially to establish a creative atmosphere of silence and solitude that would free the spirit for contemplative grace. No one knew better than Teresa that contemplation is a gift of God, freely given – and that it is more often rejected than withheld. She was fully aware of just how great God's desire is to grant this grace to those who prepare themselves for it and are willing to pay the price.

Contemplative prayer takes possession of the human heart, awakening *a little spark of the Lord's true love which He begins to enkindle in the soul* (L 15:4); it opens the heart to the transforming, radiant presence hidden in the soul's innermost castle. Nothing in the universe is more intensely alive and active than contemplative prayer. It is a gift received sometimes in joy; often in pain and dereliction of spirit – God moulding and shaping the soul in the image and likeness of Christ.

There is nothing small or narrow about Teresa's understanding of contemplative prayer. It is a burning reality at the heart of the Church; it transcends categories, just as she herself did. The contemplative gaze penetrates to the heart of all human reality; it is the deepest source of energy and compassion for a world in need. The essence of prayer lies not in ideas or the imagination, not in mystical favours or extraordinary graces, but in genuine love and unselfish service: *This is the reason for prayer...: the birth always of good works, good works* (IC VII:4:6).

A daughter of the Church

It is impossible to understand Teresa's teaching on prayer without stressing the importance of contemplative prayer in the life of the Church. She felt the pain of a Church that was losing its way in a sea of controversy and disunity. She was a true daughter of the Church, and her life was totally given to its service. As her friendship with the Lord increased, so too did her desire to see him better loved and better served.

The Carmelite Reform was born out of this desire. She saw prayer as a sharing in Christ's own prayer of intercession for the Church. Teresa loved the Church but was only too aware of its frailty. It was, for the most part, a tragic, broken and sinful Church that she encountered; yet of its holiness and essential mystery she had no doubt. She wished to serve it in whatever way she could: *I tried to please the Lord with my poor prayers and always endeavoured that the Sisters would do the same and dedicate themselves to the good of souls and the increase of His Church* (F 1:6).

Despite the many extraordinary favours Teresa herself received, she is adamant that the essence of contemplative prayer is not to be found in them. The test – the only test – is the awakening of a true and genuine love for God, and an unselfish service of others with compassion and care: *let us desire and be occupied in prayer not for the sake of our enjoyment but so as to have this strength to serve* (IC VII:4:12). For Teresa, it was only a heart wounded with love and with yearnings for God that could help heal a broken world, and purify a tired and fractured Church.

4. Prayer and life

Teresa's whole spirituality pulsates with a vibrant and dynamic realism, firmly rooted in the practicalities of everyday living. For all her visions and ecstasies, she knew how to find the Lord *among the pots and pans* (F 5:8); in fact, her skill in the kitchen was just as great as her skill at prayer!

One of the pillars of Teresian spirituality is the relationship between prayer and life. How we pray depends on how we live; our life, in turn, is a reflection of the way we pray. In Teresa's scheme of things, there is not only a relationship, there is interdependence: prayer, not tested by life, is suspect; life, not nourished by prayer, is of little value.

Teresa often speaks about virtue as the *current coin,...unfailing revenue* (WP 18:7): its value is never diminished and, in the end, it is the only real test of authentic prayer. Prayer and virtue both demand faithfulness and perseverance. Daily life is the place where authenticity of prayer is proved: *I would not want any other prayer than that which makes the virtues grow in me* (Lt 136:5). Prayer is life lived faithfully, day by day, in the light of the gospel call. It must reveal itself in action: *It benefits me little to be alone making acts of devotion to our Lord, proposing and promising to do wonders in His service, if I then go away and when the occasion offers itself do everything the opposite* (IC VII:4:7).

All her teaching in *The Way of Perfection* about the prayer of recollection highlights the fact that we can, with a little effort, achieve the necessary control over our thoughts and imagination to allow us to rest quietly and attentively in the presence of God – and thus grow in virtue and readiness to serve.

Walking in the truth

No matter how beautiful or moving any experience in prayer may be, it is always suspect if it does not lead ultimately to goodness of life: *the love of God does not consist in tears or in this delight and tenderness…but it consists in serving with justice and fortitude of soul and in humility* (L 11:13).

Both in her selection and her description of virtue, we see the concrete and practical dimension of her spirituality. She does not give a long list of virtues but focuses on three. These are social and relational: *I shall enlarge on only three things… The first of these is love for one another; the second is detachment from all created things; the third is true humility, which, even though I speak of it last, is the main practice and embraces all the others* (WP 4:4). If the soul possesses these, it is mistress of itself and slave to none save God: *these are the virtues I desire you to have,…the ones you must strive for* (WP 18:9).

Teresa writes with great insight about each of these, obviously the fruit of her own lived experience. Her advice is well tailored to the domestic problems of community living and to the vacillations and evasions of human nature. Mutual love shows itself in a practical concern for others – gentle, supportive and compassionate: *all must be friends, all must be loved, all must be held dear, all must be helped* (WP 4:7). Detachment shows itself in freedom of spirit, an indispensable quality for maturity and personal growth, and *if it is practised with perfection, [it] includes everything* (WP 8:1).

Basically, this is a living out of the gospel beatitude of 'poverty of spirit', acknowledging our dependence on God and confidently trusting in him. Yet there is no doubt that, for Teresa, humility is the queen of all virtues – *the ointment for our wounds* (IC III:2:6). It is the foundation, the bedrock, of the whole spiritual life: *What I have come to understand is that this whole groundwork of prayer is based on humility* (L 2:11). She draws on the idea of a game of chess, saying that humility alone can give checkmate to the King (cf. WP 16:1-2). It has nothing to do with loss of self-esteem; on the contrary, *to be humble is to walk in truth* (IC VI:10:7). It is about authenticity and honesty, and puts the seal of truth on the way we live. It is about being satisfied with what is given us, and rejoicing in the truth about ourselves and others. It goes hand in hand with genuine self-knowledge, which is the *bread with which all palates must be fed* (L 13:15).

5. *All glorious within*

The beauty and capacity of the human soul was a source of constant wonder and never-ending joy for Teresa. We know she often discussed it with her directors and the theologians with whom she spoke. She admits she cannot ultimately find anything with which to compare it. The whole reality being a matter of faith, we will no more be able to attain to an understanding of it, than we will of God himself. Yet, for all that, she never ceased to try.

How beautifully simple are her words: *the soul of the just person is nothing else but a paradise where the Lord says He finds His delight* (IC I:1:1). Few have been so privileged to experience the mystery of the human soul in such a personal and intimate way, and few have managed so successfully to communicate this experience to others. All her writings attest to the familiarity with which she moved in the sphere of the spirit, and the clarity with which she recorded her experiences.

We must not look to Teresa for clear definitions or precise terminology. She is not a theologian but a mystic. Her witness is in the realm of experience, an experience that was essentially personal and dynamic. Teresa's relationship with the spiritual world was never purely passive or receptive. Rather, it was part of that vital exchange and relationship of love, intimacy and boldness that characterised all her dealings with the divine. There was nothing abstract about her experience of grace: quite simply, it was God's own communication of himself to her in love – God himself, in a vital and personal way, making his presence more real and more creative within her soul.

Teresa's understanding of God's life within her was one of endless activity and a constant source of wonder – he was the Sun ever shining, the living fountain that never ceased to flow, the radiant presence that illumined her soul in its innermost centre, ceaselessly drawing her to ever deeper union and transformation. To speak of grace is to speak of God's activity within, and of the gradual radiation of his presence across the whole spectrum of our life and personality.

The divine company

How profound Teresa's experience of God was ultimately to become is something she could never have imagined as she made those first steps across the threshold of the castle. She had lived for many years in the intimate awareness of Christ's personal presence in her life. Now it was all changed utterly – suddenly transformed and transfigured by an overwhelming realisation of the presence of the Trinity revealed within: *It seemed to me...my soul...was overflowing with that divinity and in a certain way rejoicing within itself and possessing the three Persons* (ST 14).

This experience would often be repeated and intensified over the last years of her life; a truth that overwhelmed her soul as *sponge absorbs and is saturated with water* (ST 14), and she bore the reality of the divine persons *imprinted in [her] soul* (ST 42). Breathless with amazement, she struggled for words: *Oh, God help me! How different is hearing and believing these words from understanding their truth in this way! Each day this soul becomes more amazed... in some place very deep within itself,...it perceives this divine company* (IC VII:1:7).

In many ways, this is her ultimate testimony and the defining goal of her mystical experiences. It stands in a unique place in the history of spiritual theology, an unparalleled witness to the central truth of revelation: *Here all three Persons communicate themselves to [the soul]...and explain those words of the Lord in the Gospel: that He and the Father and the Holy Spirit will come to dwell with the soul that loves Him and keeps His commandments* (IC VII:1:6).

6. *Determined determination*

Teresa begins the story of her life with this poignant lament: *if I had not been so wretched...* (L 1:1); and this insistence on her own infidelities and resistance to God's grace runs like a refrain through her writings. Already, in the Prologue to her *Life*, she remarks: *I made a study out of resisting the favours His Majesty was granting me* (L Prol. 1). She never hides or excuses her infidelities – compromises, backsliding, tepidity of soul; they are all recorded, not with any false rhetoric or even out of humility, but simply to proclaim, to all, the utter gratuitousness of God's grace and to magnify him for his mercies. Indeed, it was only under the weight of immense spiritual favours that her bold, independent spirit and her strong, vigorous personality finally yielded to the moulding action of the divine Artist.

Conversion is no small grace for Teresa. It is a great thing to be a beginner – to start again, to take spiritual realities seriously, and to renew our personal commitment to God: *There is no stage of prayer so sublime that it isn't necessary to return often to the beginning* (L 13:15). She knew the importance of encouragement, and used her natural charm and gifts of persuasion to inspire others to make that basic commitment to the Lord that often needs only the first step. We see her at her best in those early chapters of *The Way of Perfection*, where she is encouraging her sisters not to withdraw from the path of perfection. *They must have a great and very resolute determination to persevere until reaching the end, come what may, happen what may, whatever work is involved, whatever criticism arises,...or if the whole world collapses* (WP 21:2).

Gently, with motherly care, she speaks of the advantages of perseverance, the importance of generosity of heart, and the need for real determination. Such dispositions, she assures them, far outweigh in their benefits any little effort or hardship required on their part. She makes the difficult seem easy and accessible, because she knows from her own experience that, once this resolve is there, everything else will follow.

Such fortitude is a linchpin of Teresa's teaching: *determined determination* (WP 21:2), she literally called it. It affects every aspect of our relationship with God and with others. For Teresa, always practical and realistic, it especially means perseverance in prayer and in the following of Christ. Without this real and absolute determination to give oneself to prayer, there can be no real progress or stability in the spiritual life: *I don't think losing the way means anything else than giving up prayer* (L 19:12). And without prayer, there can be no authentic living of the Christian life.

Teresa herself admits that the Lord seemed to have given her more courage than he did to most women; and although she laments the fact that she did not use it well, others would not agree with her. Born into a family of conquistadors and a true daughter of 'Avila of the Knights', there was about her a certain resoluteness and spirit of adventure that could inspire others. She wanted her nuns to acquit themselves like good and faithful soldiers, *convinced of how important victory is and that... to conquer is to live* (WP 23:5).

There was nothing small or cautious about Teresa: she was not afraid to take a risk or to step out in faith despite seemingly impossible obstacles. But, for all that, there was nothing foolhardy about her decisions. Her trust and confidence were firmly rooted in the Lord, or in 'His Majesty', as she liked to call him. In his service difficulties were a spur to action, and she went wherever he called, regardless of challenges or obstacles.

Undaunted daughter of desires

Finally, linked with her emphasis on determination and on wholehearted service of the Lord, is Teresa's insistence on the importance of great desires. Named by the poet Crashaw 'undaunted daughter of desires', she knew just how necessary it is to want to achieve great things for God: *I marvel at how important it is to be courageous in striving for great things along this path* (L 13:2) – though she also said, humorously, to Padre Gracián: *I enjoyed the account of the crossing of the Red Sea, thinking of how much less it is that we are asking for* (Lt 128:4)!

Without desire, the soul is earth-bound – going along, as she so graphically expresses it, *at the speed of a hen* (L 13:5)! She urges directors not to allow the sisters to be like *toads* or merely to show them *how to catch little lizards* (L 13:3)! It is not that every desire will be fulfilled; but it is by our yearnings and our desires that God draws us to himself and lifts us to greater heights. Desires are the measure of our love and confidence in God. The more we reach out to him in hope, the more his power can work in and through us.

Postscript

Teresa of Avila is certainly one of the great women of history. She has too many claims to fame to be otherwise – a writer, a reformer, a foundress, a saint, and a Doctor of the Church. But her influence, like her personality, is larger than life and stretches beyond time. Whether we read her for the clarity of her teaching or the freshness of her prose, her writings have a remarkable charm, and they contain that universal and transcendent quality that belongs to all time.

Without doubt, Teresa of Avila is a 'woman of genius' in her life, in her achievements, and in her writings. But she is also, as Kate O'Brien so aptly observes, a 'dangerous fellow creature'[21] – dangerous indeed, perhaps even subversive. Not only does Teresa challenge our way of thinking. She can also profoundly change – and ultimately transform – the way in which we live. And she lives on today in her writings. Her presence is still vibrant and luminous; and through them we are enriched by her wisdom, her humanity, and a universal message of hope.

Teresa's writings open up for us the world of the spirit – for many, a place largely unknown and unexplored – where God is real, living and personal. She reveals a world of exquisite beauty and vast horizons, an interior castle of the soul where, for those willing to take the risk, a prodigious spiritual adventure can take place. For Teresa, it is God alone who can give meaning and purpose to each human life. In the end, nothing matters except to discover the reality of this truth.

Despite all her reluctance and her protests that she was only a woman, with little learning and less ability, she created out of her writings something new and beautiful for God. Her brilliance and her humility have given to the world a treasure trove of literary and spiritual gems. The genius of her indomitable spirit illumines every page.

The writings of St Teresa are a peerless gift, perhaps her greatest gift to the world and to humanity. A woman of genius, she opens up new horizons, and through the power of her words invites all who read them to risk the greatest of all adventures and to celebrate life to the full.

Notes

1. A few of these studies are listed under 'Further Reading' at the end of this book.
2. Jean-Jacques Antier, *Teresa of Ávila: God Alone Suffices*, Boston, MA: Pauline Books & Media, 2007, p. xii.
3. Editor's note, in *The Letters of St Teresa of Jesus*, vol. 2, tr. E Allison Peers, London: Sheed & Ward, 1980, p. 611, note 2 (referring to Teresa's letter to Padre Pablo Hernández, October 4, 1578).
4. From the editor's introduction to *The Interior Castle*, in *The Complete Works of Saint Teresa of Jesus*, vol. 2, ed. & tr. E Allison Peers, London: Sheed & Ward, 1946, p. 189.
5. E Allison Peers, *Mother of Carmel: A Portrait of St. Teresa of Jesus*, London: SCM Press Ltd, 1945, p. 39 (hardback edition) / p. 46 (paperback edition).
6. Teresia Renata Posselt, OCD, *Edith Stein: The Life of a Philosopher and Carmelite*, Washington, DC: ICS Publications, 2005, p. 63.
7. As differing titles and numbers are referred to by various authors on Teresa, it could be helpful to clarify the situation here. There are sixty-seven entries in the Spanish edition of Padre Silverio (which is the one followed by the English

translation of E Allison Peers); sixty-five in that of Tomás Alvarez (the one used by the ICS translation which is followed in this book). The main overall difference is that while ICS (following Tomás Alvarez) presents all the '*Spiritual Testimonies*' in chronological order, E Allison Peers (following Padre Silverio) divides his '*Spiritual Relations*' into two separate sections: the six longest entries, which he calls '*Relations*', and the sixty-one shorter ones, '*Favours of God*'. The six '*Relations*' correspond to ST 1, 2, 3, 58, 59 and 65. Apart from those six entries, the *Favours of God* and the other *Spiritual Testimonies* follow the same order (with the exception of ST 35, dated later than ST 36 but placed before it because of the subject matter). The difference in quantity (sixty-seven or sixty-five entries) arises because ST 13 combines SR 16 and 17, and ST 36 comprises SR 39 and 40.

8. In Rodolphe Hoornaert, *Saint Teresa in her Writings*, London: Sheed & Ward, 1931, p. 223.

9. *Ibid.*, p. 259.

10. See Otilio Rodríguez, OCD, *The Teresian Gospel: An Introduction to a Fruitful Reading of The Way of Perfection*, Darlington Carmel, 1993. The quotation comes from his Introduction (p. 4), where he explains his choice of title for the book.

11. See *Lumen Gentium* (*Dogmatic Constitution on the Church*), # 39-42.

12. It is considered to have been written probably

at the end of 1566 or the beginning of 1567: see Tomás Alvarez, OCD, *St. Teresa of Avila: 100 Themes on Her Life and Work*, Washington, DC: ICS Publications, 2011, p. 314; previously, the suggested date was 1569.

13. These are the words of Teresa as paraphrased by Fr Diego de Yepes, after a conversation in which she described to him how she came to write *The Interior Castle*: quoted in the editor's introduction to *The Interior Castle*, in *The Complete Works of Saint Teresa of Jesus*, vol. 2, ed. & tr. E Allison Peers, *op. cit.*, p. 188.

14. It excludes the first foundation of the Reform: St Joseph's, Avila, already described in L 32-36. Also omitted is Granada, the penultimate foundation made during Teresa's lifetime, as this was founded (in 1582) by John of the Cross and Anne of Jesus, at a time when Teresa herself was making the foundation at Burgos.

15. Alvarez, *St. Teresa of Avila*, *op. cit.*, p. 299.

16. Cf. E Allison Peers, *Saint Teresa of Jesus and other Essays and Addresses*, London: Faber and Faber, 1953, p. 118.

17. *Depositions of the Process of St. Teresa of Jesus*, Flemington, NJ: Carmel of Flemington, 1969, p. 45.

18. Alvarez, *St. Teresa of Avila*, *op. cit.*, p. 378.

19. There are four hundred and sixty-eight letters that have come down to us. Lt 6-Lt 468 come from the years 1568 to 1582; there are no surviving

letters written in 1567, the year Teresa founded the convent of Medina del Campo.

20. This was a figure of the *ecce homo*, rather than a statue of Christ at the pillar as is sometimes thought. See *The Collected Works of St. Teresa of Avila*, vol. 1, trs. Kieran Kavanaugh, OCD & Otilio Rodriguez, OCD, Washington, DC: ICS Publications, 1987, p. 471.

21. Kate O'Brien, *Teresa of Avila*, Cork & Dublin: Mercier Press, 1951, p. 9.

Abbreviations and Editions Used

The translation and paragraph numbering used in this book for the writings of St Teresa are taken from the following editions of her works:

The Collected Works of St. Teresa of Avila, 3 vols., trs. Kieran Kavanaugh, OCD & Otilio Rodriguez, OCD, Washington, DC: ICS Publications, 1987, 1980 & 1985.

The Collected Letters of St. Teresa of Avila, 2 vols., tr. Kieran Kavanaugh, OCD, Washington, DC: ICS Publications, 2001 & 2007.

The following abbreviations are used in referring to her works:

L	*The Book of Her Life*
ST	*Spiritual Testimonies*
WP	*The Way of Perfection*
IC	*The Interior Castle*
F	*The Book of Her Foundations*
M	*Meditations on the Song of Songs*

MV	*On Making the Visitation*
C	*The Constitutions*
Sol	*Soliloquies*
RSC	*Response to a Spiritual Challenge*
Sat Cri	*A Satirical Critique*
P	Poems
Lt	Letters

Further Reading

The first group of works in this selection give an overview of Teresa's life and writings; the second is on individual works by Teresa. Most of the following books are available, but older studies of particular note have also been included.

Studies on Teresa's Life and Writings

Tomás Alvarez, OCD, *St. Teresa of Avila: 100 Themes on Her Life and Work*, Washington, DC: ICS Publications, 2011. (See especially pp. 219-64 on Teresa as a writer, and pp. 265-407 on the writings of Teresa.)

Rodolphe Hoornaert, *Saint Teresa in her Writings*, London: Sheed & Ward, 1931.

E Allison Peers, *Mother of Carmel: A Portrait of St. Teresa of Jesus*, London: SCM Press Ltd, 1945.

E Allison Peers, *Saint Teresa of Jesus and other Essays and Addresses*, London: Faber and Faber, 1953.

Sebastian V Ramge, OCD, *An Introduction to the Writings of Saint Teresa*, Chicago, IL: Henry Regnery Company, 1963.

Tessa Bielecki, *Teresa of Avila: An Introduction to her Life and Writings*, Tunbridge Wells: Burns & Oates, 1994.

Rowan Williams, *Teresa of Avila*, London & New York: Continuum, 1991.

Peter Tyler, *Teresa of Avila: Doctor of the Soul*, London: Bloomsbury, 2013.

Joseph F Chorpenning, OSFS, *The Divine Romance: Teresa of Ávila's Narrative Theology*, Chicago, IL: Loyola University Press, 1992.

Elizabeth Hamilton, *The Life of Saint Teresa of Ávila*, Wheathampstead: Anthony Clarke, 1982. (First published as *The Great Teresa*, London: Chatto & Windus, 1960.)

Deirdre Green, *Gold in the Crucible: Teresa of Avila and the Western Mystical Tradition*, Longmead, Shaftesbury: Element Books, 1989.

Studies on Individual Works by Teresa

The Book of Her Life

For discussions of the *Life*, see the relevant chapters in the studies listed above.

The Way of Perfection

Kieran Kavanaugh, OCD, *St. Teresa of Avila: The Way of Perfection – A Study Edition*, Washington, DC: ICS Publications, 2000.

Otilio Rodríguez, OCD, *The Teresian Gospel: An Introduction to a Fruitful Reading of The Way of Perfection*, Darlington Carmel, 1993.

Jerome Lantry, OCD, *St Teresa on Prayer: Exploring The Way of Perfection*, forthcoming with Teresian Press in 2014.

Aloysius Rego, OCD, *The Our Father: St Teresa of Avila's Catechism of Prayer*, forthcoming with Teresian Press in 2014.

The Interior Castle

Kieran Kavanaugh, OCD & Carol Lisi, OCDS, *St. Teresa of Avila: The Interior Castle – Study Edition*, Washington, DC: ICS Publications, 2010.

Ruth Burrows, *Interior Castle Explored: St Teresa's Teaching on the Life of Deep Union with God*, London: Burns & Oates, 2007.

Julienne McLean, *Towards Mystical Union: A Modern Commentary on the Mystical Text The Interior Castle by St Teresa of Avila*, 2nd edition [revised], London: St Pauls, 2013.

Susan Muto, *Where Lovers Meet: Inside the Interior Castle*, Washington, DC: ICS Publications, 2008.

Gillian T W Ahlgren, *Entering Teresa of Avila's Interior Castle: A Reader's Companion*, New York & Mahwah, NJ: Paulist Press, 2005.

Peter Bourne, HMC, *St. Teresa's Castle of the Soul: A Study of the Interior Castle*, Long Beach, CA: Wenzel Press, 1995.

Vilma Seelaus, OCD, *Distractions in Prayer: Blessing or Curse? – St. Teresa of Avila's Teachings in The Interior Castle*, Staten Island, NY: St Pauls, 2005.

Carolyn Humphreys, OCDS, *From Ash to Fire – An Odyssey in Prayer: A Contemporary Journey through the Interior Castle of Teresa of Avila*, Hyde Park, NY: New City Press, 1992.

Eugene McCaffrey, OCD, *Journey of Love: Teresa of Avila's Interior Castle – A Reader's Guide*, forthcoming with Teresian Press in 2014.

The Book of Her Foundations

Marc Foley, OCD, *St. Teresa of Avila: The Book of Her Foundations – A Study Guide*, Washington, DC: ICS Publications, 2011.

Meditations on the Song of Songs

Kevin Culligan, OCD, *St. Teresa of Avila: Meditations on the Song of Songs – Study Edition*, forthcoming with ICS Publications in 2015.

Poetry

Eric W Vogt, *The Complete Poetry of St. Teresa of Avila: A Bilingual Edition*, New Orleans, LA: University Press of the South, 1996.

Letters

Bárbara Mujica, *Teresa de Ávila: Lettered Woman*, Nashville, TN: Vanderbilt University Press, 2009.

TERESIAN PRESS
SOME FORTHCOMING PUBLICATIONS

St Teresa on Prayer: Exploring The Way of Perfection .
Jerome Lantry, OCD

Living with God: St Teresa's Understanding of Prayer
Tomás Álvarez, OCD

A Moment of Prayer – A Life of Prayer
Conrad De Meester, OCD

The Our Father: St Teresa of Avila's Catechism of Prayer
Aloysius Rego, OCD

*Captive Flames: A Biblical Reading of
the Carmelite Saints – **to be reissued***
James McCaffrey, OCD

*Journey of Love: Teresa of Avila's Interior Castle
– A Reader's Guide*
Eugene McCaffrey, OCD

What Carmel Means to Me
Edited by James McCaffrey, OCD & Joanne Mosley

Teresian Press
Carmelite Priory
Boars Hill
Oxford OX1 5HB

www.carmelitebooks.com